THOUGHTS
BECOME
THINGS

Change Your Thoughts...
Change Your World

JO BANKS

First Edition: November 2015

Published by What Next? Media

ISBN: 978-0-9934445-0-0

For my Dad...

I love you.

"Your beliefs become your thoughts,

Your thoughts become your words,

Your words become your actions,

Your actions become your habits,

Your habits become your values,

Your values become your destiny."

Mahatma Gandhi

CONTENTS

FOREWORD

"What you think about comes about"

Hello and welcome to my first book. I'm excited to finally share the tools and techniques that I've been successfully using with my clients for years. My style of coaching is focused around enabling my clients to make quick but long lasting changes. Although I do coach some clients over many years, my average number of sessions for a client who has a particular issue such as confidence, mild depression, anxiety, stress, overwhelm, underperformance and general 'unhappiness' etc, is usually between two to four sessions.

I'm a coach and not a therapist. However, I do help people identify their unhelpful thinking patterns (which are the cause of most of our problems) and help them change quickly. I'm not a fan of prolonged therapy i.e. making someone sit in a chair week after

1

week asking them about their history and background and then sending them off with big gaping wounds with no idea of how to heal them (although I'm sure it must work some of the time). What I do know is that 'talking therapy' works very well for the therapist who gets paid, week after week, year after year, even in the absence of any clear results! That makes no sense to me whatsoever and I've seen it do much more harm than good. I want to help my clients now, immediately, not in six months or two years time.

In order to do this, I've developed a toolkit based on principles taken from my formal training in NLP (Neurolinguistic Programming), CBT (Cognitive Behavioural Therapy) and EFT (Emotional Freedom Technique) plus ideas and principles gained from reading over 400 self development and business books. As well as using information gained from attending countless workshops and seminars in the field of human and business development.

Throughout the years, I've tried many techniques both on me and with my clients and have now honed my toolkit to include only what I know really works. It's this information that I share with my clients and what I'm now sharing with you in this book. Nothing has been included here that hasn't been tried and tested many times ... THIS STUFF WORKS!

MY COACHING PRACTICE

I've coached approximately 1500 people since I set up my business What Next Consultancy (www.whatnextconsultancy.co.uk) nearly seven years ago and have coached countless more during my twenty years as a Senior Human Resources Professional. Working with so many different people with different upbringings, backgrounds, ages, careers, religions etc, would have meant I was worryingly unobservant had I not noticed that there were certain patterns in our thinking and behaviour that affect our ability to achieve the lives we really want and deserve. It's these thoughts, emotions and behaviours that I'll be addressing throughout the book.

You may notice that I've repeated some things a number of times, that's because those things are important for you to understand, learn and put into practise. You may also find that there is just one small thing that resonates with you and that causes you to take some sort of action as a result. All great change starts with the first thought, so any action you take as a result of reading this book, will set a course set in motion that could change your life forever, that is my intention for you.

"STOP TRYING TO HELP PEOPLE"

That's something my mum once said to me ... my mum! To say

3

we've had a turbulent relationship is an understatement. I had quite a difficult childhood and I think it's important to share a little of it, so that you understand that we *can* change what's not working and that *the past does not equal the future*. We have control over our destiny, but only if we take responsibility for how our lives have turned out, make the decision to change what we don't like or what's not working and continue to take consistent action until we see the results we want.

My mother was raised in a strict Methodist household with a controlling, authoritative Victorian style father and a meek and mild mother (my mum and her siblings were controlled to such an extent that they had to count how many times they chewed their food - twenty times - before they were allowed to swallow). Through that controlled upbringing, my mother (I know now) learnt a very 'off-centre' way of looking at the world and developed an acute need to control everyone and everything around her.

Sadly, whoever she can't control is punished (using classic passive aggressive techniques – her favourite is taking to her bed for days on end) until they come back under her control or they are unceremoniously cut off never to been seen/heard or mentioned of again. On top of all of this, she is without a doubt THE most negative person I've ever met, without exception.

Growing up was difficult, not only did I have my mother's negativity and an absent father to deal with (my father, although he lived with us, was very rarely home - he worked for himself, putting in incredibly long hours trying to make ends meet) who also shared my mother's negativity (although not quite to the same extent). My brother hated me pretty much for as long as I can remember and we would have vicious fights often ending up with me being battered and bruised.

We lived in a fairly affluent area. However, we could only be described as poor, which was uncomfortable when my school friends were largely quite wealthy. This I now know led to my feelings of inadequacy, of never feeling like I was good enough and not really fitting in, as well as growing feelings of low self-esteem.

Unfortunately, growing up in such a negative environment with no positive role models is likely to have a negative effect on you; on your values, beliefs and rules and how you think and behave. We're all programmed as we grow by modelling the behaviours of our primary care-givers (we'll cover this in detail in Chapter 1). Sadly, right up until my thirties I fully embraced and lived with the negative values, beliefs and rules programmed in to me by my parents, not even realising that there was an alternative.

I happened to 'fall' into a career in Human Resources in my

twenties and despite my ongoing negativity, through hard work and determination; I managed to progress to a senior level reasonably quickly. However, I hated it - I disliked pretty much everything about it (if you like people, HR isn't the profession for you!). Towards the end of my last permanent HR role I was working around eighty hours a week, approximately forty of which were spent in full time union negotiations (that's a whole other book in itself - I learnt a lot about human behaviours during that time). Working in that environment was extremely negative and draining, especially for someone like me who dislikes confrontation and avoids it at all costs – I definitely learnt that behaviour from my parents. After a while it really began to take its toll on me.

My personal life was also beset with disaster after disaster and I always wondered why such awful things kept happening to me. What was I doing so wrong? My friends would often say, "We don't know how you manage to keep picking yourself up! How does someone keep coming back from such adversity?"

My default response was to blame someone or something else and I'd beat myself up on a regular basis for being such a failure. I truly saw myself as an unlucky person, not knowing at that point that we're responsible for our lives through the decisions we make and the actions we take, what I really was, was a Victim.

HOW I CHANGED MY LIFE...

All that changed the day I read Paul McKenna's 'Change your Life in 7 days'. That book actually did for me exactly what it says on the cover. I worked through it systematically as instructed and it actually did change my life forever and set me on a very different life destiny.

I finally saw that *I* was responsible for my life and that it was in my control to change it. This was a revelation to me. At first, it was extremely difficult to come to terms with the fact that my life was my fault, that *I* was the common denominator for everything that had gone 'wrong'. I had to do quite a bit of soul searching to make sense of it and I did end up in quite a downward spiral for a while afterwards. However, once I did come to terms with it, nothing would ever be the same again.

From that moment, over 10 years ago, when I read that book, I've never looked back. Since then, as I mentioned previously, I've read hundreds of books within the human potential field, I qualified as a Neuro Linguistic Programming Master Practitioner (NLP), a Cognitive Behavioural Therapist (CBT), and I've formally studied many other systems including   Emotional Freedom Technique (EFT), Executive Coaching, Mindfulness, Hypnotherapy, Emotional Intelligence and Body Language to mention but a few.

7

I've attended numerous courses and workshops with some of the world's greatest coaches, authors and thinkers in the self-development field today, including Anthony Robbins, Richard Bandler (the co-creator of NLP), Paul McKenna, Michael Neill, and Robert Holden amongst many others. I'm on a constant quest to find the very best techniques that will help both my clients and myself be the best we can be.

Thankfully, I ignored my mother and her instruction to "Stop helping people!" I did stop trying to help her however and I've now dedicated my life to helping others to achieve the life they deserve. Having such a negative upbringing and now knowing that life can be so different, spurs me on to get the message out there. As a result, I've now gone on to help a significant number of people gain control of their lives and I intend to do so for as long as I'm able.

My life is so different now, I hardly recognise myself. I attribute this transformation to my change in thinking and my willingness to take RESPONSIBILITY and take consistent ACTION. I won't deny that I still have my challenges and some days are easier than others. However, on the whole, my life is unrecognisable from how it was 10 years ago ... I'm finally happy and my point in sharing my story with you is that no matter what's happened to you in the past, YOU CAN BE HAPPY TOO!

THERE'S ALWAYS SOMETHING YOU CAN DO

2012 was without doubt one of the hardest twelve months of my life and despite my continued optimism, it remained incredibly difficult throughout. I now describe it as my 'Mad Year'. I won't go into the details of what happened, suffice to say that my business and personal relationships were all failing miserably. Despite my taking consistent positive action, nothing seemed to work and I was moving quickly towards losing everything I had worked so hard to create.

When you're going through difficult times, it's hard to see the reasons for it. Even for the most positive of people, there can be a tendency to think, "Why me?", and that's certainly where I was, especially towards the end of the year when things were looking particularly grim. It seriously caused me to question and challenge all of my newfound thoughts, ideas, values, and beliefs.

Looking back, I can see the positives in having gone through what I did. I'm now a true believer that everything happens for a reason, that your actions today create your future and there are always things to learn from even the most difficult of circumstances. After all, if you just tootled on day after day without anything ever changing, you would never grow and develop, which I think is the whole reason why we're here.

I've learnt some incredibly hard and sometimes painful lessons over the course of my life, many of which I experienced during that 12 months, and my hope in sharing what I've discovered, is for you to realise that you're not on your own and that there are always things you can do, no matter how difficult you think your situation is.

Here are just a few of the most important lessons I've learnt...

WHAT YOU THINK ABOUT COMES ABOUT

I thought I knew all there was to know about the law of attraction (in its simplest terms, *you get what you think about*) but I didn't quite anticipate how it delivers your worst fears as well as your desires, quite as well as it does. Therefore, embracing not just positive thinking but a positive outlook is THE most important thing you can do for yourself. Having a positive outlook changes everything and allows you to get through even the most difficult of times much more effectively and brings more positivity to you - *like attracts like*.

YOU ALWAYS FIND A WAY THROUGH

No matter what happens to you in life, no matter how hard things get or how low you feel, *you will always find a way through*. It might be tough when you're in the middle of it and you may find it difficult to make sense of what's happening, but there is always a solution to everything. You just need to *dig deep, ask the right QUESTIONS, make good DECISIONS and take consistent ACTION* (you'll hear me saying that many times throughout the book).

'WORRY IS FUTILE'

Living through adversity makes me believe this statement with absolute certainty. Worry is such a useless emotion, which gets you worked up about things that may never happen and that aren't even real. Worry saps your ability to reason, your strength and the capacity to think your problems through rationally. Whatever *actually* happens, you can deal with it, and you can always find a way through, whereas it's always difficult, if not impossible, to see a way through your imagined scenarios. What you imagine can be far more terrifying than anything that could actually happen. Have a contingency plan by all means, but then let it go...

YOU CAN'T ALWAYS RELY ON YOUR OLDEST FRIENDS

I found that it isn't necessarily your oldest friends that will be there for you when you're truly in need. I found that help came not from those whom I'd have expected, but from people that I'd never have imagined. It's easy to think that your friends move and grow at the same rate as you do. However, that's not always the case and you may find that when the chips are down, their path has taken them to such a different place than yours that they can no longer empathise with you and your current situation. That's no reflection on either of you; it's just part of the natural change process and how we grow individually as people.

EVERYTHING HAPPENS FOR A REASON

During my Mad Year, I had some coaching sessions with Brad Yates (a leading figure in the EFT world). I explained some of the things that had happened and asked for his opinion as to what it could all mean. His take on my situation was, "How can you help people as a coach if you've never been through tough times or adversity yourself? It's all about the lessons you need to learn" I now have no doubt that everything happens for a reason.

You can't always see it at the time, but if you look hard enough at any situation after it's happened, you will (if you're honest with yourself) see the lessons that you needed to learn. I also believe that if you don't learn the lesson intended, that situation will occur again and again or the same people will keep turning up in your life, until you do.

I'm happy to say that I've come through many trials and tribulations in my life and although I'd be crazy to think that I won't hit tough times again in the future, I now know for certain that whatever happens to me I'll always be OK. I have everything within me that I need to get through whatever comes my way.

LIFE IS A SERIES OF LESSONS

In conclusion, I think life is a series of lessons that once learnt allow us to move on. If we don't learn the lesson, the same thing keeps happening until we do. Life is about living, learning, and changing the things that aren't working until you find something that does. One of my favourite sayings is, *"Always do what you've always done, always get what you've always got!"* For me, I'm removing doubt, I'm removing worry and as much negativity from my life as I possibly can and will continue with what I consider to be my life purpose:

TO HELP AS MANY PEOPLE AS I POSSIBLY CAN TO ACHIEVE A BETTER LIFE

FREEBIES

As a way of thanking you for purchasing this book, I have a number of free resources available for you, designed to complement the learning described in this book.

Visit **www.thoughtsbecomethings.co.uk** and sign up with a quality email address in order to receive regular updates and an assortment of useful tools and information to help you achieve the life you deserve.

Signing up will add you to our exclusive group of like-minded individuals, wishing to grow and change their lives for the better, head over to the website now!

www.thoughtsbecomethings.co.uk

INTRODUCTION

"The great thing about life is that you get to start again with every new day"

GETTING THE MOST OUT OF THIS BOOK

Some elements of this book will appeal to you more than others and whilst I do advocate that you read the whole book in its entirety (you never know where the 'ah-ha' or 'light bulb' moment will come from), you may wish to go straight to the section that relates most closely to your current circumstances.

I often read books a number of times and I find that I'll see the information that's pertinent to my current situation upon further reading, that I may have totally missed previously. I firmly believe that information and help comes to us when we need it the most. However, we have to be open to it and accept the 'nudge' when it comes. I also recommend that you use this book as a reference point, revisiting sections as and when an issue arises.

When I read a book or go to a seminar, my philosophy is that if I get one useable piece of information that makes me think or act differently because of it, it was worth the price. Therefore, if you get one thing from this book that makes a positive difference in your life, then I've achieved my goal (although I do hope you get far more than one!).

WHAT YOU WILL LEARN

I've taken the most effective and easy-to-use tools, ideas and techniques from my toolkit and attempted to explain them in simple, uncomplicated terms. Here's an overview of what's included:

CHAPTER 1

In this chapter, we'll look at why your life is as it is and how taking responsibility for your life can change everything. We'll be investigating what's in your control, how to use that control effectively and let go of the things that you're thinking and doing that don't serve you.

We discover that the past doesn't equal the future, i.e. whatever's happened in the past doesn't mean that the same thing will happen again in the future. I explain what you can do to break out of the cycle of learnt negative behaviour, making significant changes within yourself that will help you to get to where you want and deserve to be.

We will take a close look at the negative programming and unhelpful learnt behaviours that were subconsciously installed in you as you grew up and what tools you can use to change them.

CHAPTER 2

We will examine at how we make sense of the world, by constantly and consistently reviewing information we receive through our senses and running it through our filters. We develop our filters throughout our lifetime and they are influenced by our parents, teachers, family, peers, colleagues, religion, race/ethnicity etc. In this section, we will explore how our filters influence our thoughts, emotions and behaviours and how they affect how we interpret and react to people and situations.

CHAPTER 3

I often hear the old saying, "You can't teach an old dog new tricks" and I'm happy to say that it's utter rubbish! It's simply a question of teaching our brains a more logical way of doing things and practising the new way until it becomes our new default. In this section, you'll discover how to do this and I'll explain the reasons why you find it difficult to stop behaviours that don't serve you, providing you with techniques that allow you to change what's not working.

You'll also discover that one small change in your behaviour can facilitate positive change in someone else, no matter how difficult your relationship may be and that by setting your intention for whatever it is you're trying to accomplish will pay dividends.

CHAPTER 4

In this chapter we will look more closely at your thoughts, where they come from, what influences them and what you can do to change them quickly and easily. We'll discover how to manage negative recurring thoughts (the type of thoughts that may be keeping you up at night). What those recurring thoughts actually mean and how your thoughts affect your emotions that in turn affect your behaviours.

You'll see how your *perception* of a situation isn't necessarily right or real but is affected by your filters i.e. how you view and interpret the world. I also talk about your inner critic (that little voice inside you that left unmanaged can become uncontrollable and destructive) what it is, where it comes from and how to tame it effectively.

CHAPTER 5

In this section, I discuss a number of other aspects that affect and influence your thinking. You'll learn how your physiology (what you do with your body) and the words that you use directly affect your emotions and how visualisation can be used to influence your mood and increase your performance.

I've also included some relaxation techniques that are quick and easy to do and that are especially effective if you suffer from anxiety, stress or overwhelm. I've also provided some top tips for getting better quality sleep (a common complaint for many people) and the benefits of exercise. I also discuss the importance of scheduling 'Me Time' – time away from everything that's just for you – together with how to manage your time more effectively.

CHAPTER 6

We look at the differences between Victims and Owners (e.g. lucky versus unlucky people) and their differentiators; the difference in their thinking, decision making and actions. We uncover 'Your Story', the story you tell yourself and others about why your life is as it is and ask the ultimate question, *"Who would you be without your story?"*

WHAT NEXT?

Finally, we will look at what's next. This section is a summary of all the key points raised in the book, together with some tips on how to put the information and lessons that you've learnt into practice.

EXERCISES

I've included a number of exercises throughout the book designed to help you understand the related section more fully and imbed your learning. I strongly urge you to try them, as research has shown that physically taking action rather than simply reading something increases your retention rate by 700%. I recommend that you read the exercises thoroughly, at least twice, before you try them so that you understand the actions you'll need to take.

HOW TO KEEP UP MOMENTUM

You may find that you start to adopt the principles described in this book with great gusto, only to find that you 'forget' to carry on implementing them after a couple of days. If that happens, don't worry, *we are always a work in progress*, simply STOP, draw a line and start again! *The great thing about life is that you get to start again with every new day.*

After all, if a child who was learning to walk fell down, you wouldn't stop it from getting up and trying again. Nothing is ever set in stone, once you have the realisation that you've slipped, don't beat yourself up, simply start again. The more you do this, the more quickly you'll notice if you do slip back into old habits and the easier it will become to notice and rectify it.

HOW TO DEAL WITH ROAD BLOCKS

It's quite common for my new clients to experience some resistance from their friends and family, when they start to implement changes. When I started on my path to rid myself of negative thinking and change my behaviours, I'd often get sarcastic comments from people around me when I said or did something that wasn't consistent with my 'old negative self'. Comments would often be cynical or sarcastic e.g., "Been on a course have you?" "Did you get that from another book?" "Stop trying to help people"!

I know now that these people had a stake in trying to stop me from changing. It's a sad fact that when you do start to transform your thinking and behaviours, anyone who resonates strongly with the 'old you' (e.g. they are a negative thinking person too) will throw up resistance for a number of reasons:

1. *They can be frightened that they'll lose you* - If you change, then you may not want to be around them anymore - that is a real threat to them because in reality, you probably won't. Therefore, they have a stake in you staying the way you are

21

so that they don't lose you.

2. *It holds a mirror up to them and makes them uncomfortable* - They see you changing, becoming happier and having a better life, but they don't want to change or they don't realise that they can and so it makes them feel uncomfortable. Their current thoughts and behaviours are serving them in some way which is usually processed in their subconscious. In NLP terms, we call this Secondary Gain which I cover in detail in Chapter 3.

3. *They become jealous of the new you and try to sabotage your progress* - This is closely related to numbers 1 and 2 in that the jealous person simply doesn't want to put the effort in that's required to change, which makes them feel bad when they see you succeeding.

   This is often the case with clients wanting to lose weight - people around them will try and tempt them with cakes and other goodies. If that's the case with you, then you need to question the other person's motives - do you think they might be trying to sabotage you and if so, why?

Now you're aware that people *may* try to sabotage you, the key is to spot it early and not to let it derail you. Keep doing what you're doing and you'll reap the rewards, learn to simply smile at them and change the subject. You may even decide at some point that you need to do a 'friend de-clutter'. As harsh as it may sound, you may need to do some pruning of your friendships and remove the more negative people from your life, if that's possible.

REMOVE NEGATIVE INFLUENCES

I've 'reviewed' my friendships a few times over the years and I can't say I've missed the people I've chosen to remove completely from my life or chosen to spend less time with. I've never regretted it, not even for a minute because those people were not really my friends; they simply hung around for their own agenda. Your true friends will support you no matter what you do, how you look, or how odd your decisions seem to them. They may offer constructive feedback, but that is very different from criticism. People who aren't true friends criticise and make you feel bad about yourself; it's as simple as that.

I often see this problem when I work with graduates. When they first start university and come home for the holidays, they can find that their friends and sometimes even family members have changed towards them. This can leave them with a range of negative emotions from bewilderment to mild depression because they don't know what they have done wrong.

What happens is that the student leaves the family home and

23

goes off to university, which often involves relocating to a new city. Their life changes almost immediately; they are surrounded by new people and are opened up to new ideas, they have to fend for themselves instead of their parents and family doing everything for them and *it changes them*! When they then come home, usually everything and everyone else has stayed the same, but *they* (the student) haven't. They have changed and that can cause resistance from friends and family.

I had one graduate client who told me that one of his best friends from school, someone whom he had grown up with and was always close to, was now treating him badly and acting aggressively towards him. He said that his friend would call him 'stuck up' and said that he had 'forgotten his roots' (his friend had decided that university wasn't for him and he got a job in his hometown as a mechanic). My client was terribly upset by it as he still considered this person to be a good friend.

When I explained the concept of 'he had changed' rather than his friend and the potential reasons for his friend's behaviour, it helped him understand and come to terms with the fact that they had grown apart and now had very different lives. They were still friends but the relationship had changed, it was therefore his decision as to whether he continued to spend time with this person or not.

This scenario affects so many graduates that I've now incorporated it into one of the workshops that form part of a year-long Graduate Leadership Development Programme that I deliver.

Sadly, this isn't a problem that just affects graduates; it can affect all of us. It's relatively easy to spot the type of people I'm talking about here. If you spend time with someone who makes you feel drained afterwards, if they monopolise the conversation and don't allow you to get a word in edgeways or if they criticise or put you down in any way, that person doesn't deserve you and they aren't a true friend.

I realise that often the most negative people around you can be your family, in that case, it's often inappropriate to cut them out of your life. However, what you can do is make a conscious decision to spend less time with them. If you absolutely have to see them, limit the number of times and the amount of time you spend with them. Just because they're family does not mean that you owe them anything and maybe it's time to start thinking more about what you want and need rather than always putting others first.

STICK WITH IT

When you come up against resistance, it often feels easier not to change but to stay as you are; after all, change takes consistent effort. However, the rewards you get when you decide and commit to making changes, will be repaid tenfold. Stick with it and remember if you forget and slip into your old patterns of thinking, it's just your old programming - **STOP, DECIDE WHAT YOU WANT AND START AGAIN!**

CHAPTER 1

"Everything we have in our lives is a result of what we have thought"

TAKE RESPONSIBLITY

THE BLAME GAME

Taking responsibility for your life is one of the most powerful things that you can do. Whether you realise it or not, whatever you have in your life right now (your relationships, your career, your possessions etc) are all a direct result of your past thoughts and actions, your current situation can't be blamed on anyone or anything else, other than yourself.

I often hear people blaming their parents, wife/husband/ partner, the economy, politicians, bosses, luck, fate and any amount of outside influences for how their lives have turned out. However, the truth is, you made the choices, you made the decisions, you took the action (or you may have taken no action at all), that got you to where you are, what you're experiencing and what you have in your life today.

If you've been playing the 'blame game', you may find this particularly difficult to hear. It isn't easy to find out that you and you alone are responsible for your life as it is now. It can be shocking to realise that your life is of your own design; after all, it's much easier to blame someone or something else.

I used to blame anyone or anything else I could think of for how 'bad' my life was. It was always 'someone else's fault', after all, that's what I'd grown up believing. I believed that we (our family) were inherently 'unlucky' and that 'only bad things ever happened to us' and that's how I lived my life. I never realised that I was 'unlucky' because I had continually negative thoughts and made terrible decisions on the back of those thoughts.

Of course, the thoughts and beliefs I had, had been directly inherited/learnt from my parents, they had literally been programmed into me whilst growing up; to such an extent that it never occurred to me that I was wrong. Even when friends would point out all the good things that I had in my life, I'd reply, "That doesn't mean anything, I'm still unlucky and I always will be - I hate my life. Why do bad things keep happening to me?"

STOP THE PITY PARTY

When I think back to all the great things that I've had in my life over the years, but I still insisted on having my own Pity Party, it makes me cringe. I can hear myself with that whiney, childlike voice saying, "Nothing good ever happens to me" - that used to be one of my main mantras and I'd say it constantly, often hundreds of times a day or my other was, "I wish I'd never been born".

If you know anything about mantras, you'll know that the more you say them, the more you believe them and the more you behave in a way that reinforces them. A good point to make here is that *we have to be consistent with our view of ourselves,* so repeating such a disabling mantra, simply made my self-pity more real and justifiable to me.

Things started to change for me once I started to take responsibility for my life and stopped making excuses and blaming others. Once you acknowledge that you're responsible for your life, you can then use that power in order to take decisive action towards achieving what you want, rather than accepting the life you *think* have been 'given'.

Self-pity happens to be one of my pet hates now; I can't bear to be around people who are self-pitying. I really have to manage my emotions when I'm with them as it provokes quite a strong negative reaction in me, probably because I know that it's not how life has to be and how disabling and 'victim' like it is.

HOW TO START TO TAKE RESPONSBILITY

Here are four ways that you can start to take responsibility for your life, starting now:

1. ***Stop being a 'People Pleaser'***

As we grow up, many of us are conditioned to become 'People Pleasers'. People Pleasers put others wants and needs before their own and tend to consider themselves to be selfless and self-sacrificing. They often have quite a distorted view of how their actions are helping others.

'Pleasers' adopt these traits subconsciously because they serve them in some way. They receive something that they subconsciously need in return for their actions/behaviour. These may include:

- Love and/or attention

- It stops them from being physically or mentally abused or generally mistreated

30

- They think it will make people like them

- It increases their self-esteem

- It makes them feel wanted and significant

The unfortunate thing with people pleasing is that when we get older, it can often become out of control and have a significant detrimental effect on the Pleaser. Long-term Pleasers tend to feel worn out, unappreciated (their actions go largely unnoticed with little thanks) which can leave them feeling isolated, unloved and unappreciated. People pleasing is often referred to as 'The Disease to Please' because of its debilitating nature.

If you recognise that you have people pleasing habits, you need first to take responsibility for your actions, after all, it's you doing the pleasing, and in my experience, *as long as you're happy to give, people are always going to be happy to take.* Unfortunately when we continue to give, it can often lead to complacency by the people who are receiving i.e. the more you give the more others expect, leaving you experiencing a series of negative emotions and feeling physically drained. Another point to note is that Pleasers rarely give unconditionally, they *expect* something in return e.g. love/attention even if they don't realise it consciously.

Whilst you're trying to please others, you please no-one; therefore, take a look at the things that you're doing right now. Are you doing them for the right reasons or simply because you think you should or others expect it of you or to get something in return? To help you start to consciously review what you're doing for others and whether it's in your best interest, here's a list of good questions to ask yourself:

- "Am I doing this because I want to or because someone expects me to?"

- "Do I really want to do this?"

- "Am I doing this because I'm expecting some sort of reward?" (e.g. to make someone like me or compliment me)

- "Am I doing this just to please someone else?"

- "If I'm doing this just to please someone else, am I OK with that?"

- "Will doing this help *me*?"

- "What do *I* get from doing this?"

I want to be clear here, I'm not saying that you should stop doing things just because it's the right or the nice thing to do.

However, if you're a Pleaser, doing things for others usually goes far beyond that, as I've said it can actually be quite damaging to your self-esteem in the long run. If you're happy with the answers to your questions, then fine, continue doing what you're doing. However, if you don't like them, then maybe it's time to learn how to say, "No".

2. *Learn to say "No"*

Learning how to say no, especially for the Pleaser, can be very difficult. We don't want to offend others; we often make up whole stories about what others will think and say about us if we say no. When I challenge clients who find it difficult to say no, the usual response is, "Whatever will they think about me? I can't possibly say no!"

We can never really know what people think about us, we're simply mind-reading (see Chapter 4 - Unhelpful Thinking Patterns) and to be happy, we need to learn not to be so obsessed with what others' think about us. A quote sums this up quite nicely is, *"What others think about you is none of your business"*.

If you want to take responsibility for your life, you *have* to learn to say "no". I can tell you that it's very unlikely that someone will die, the whole world won't come crashing down, and you might actually quite like the results. If saying no is difficult for you, I suggest that you start small, with something that's of no great importance and ask yourself the questions above. Don't apologise, for saying "no" because you don't have to apologise for taking responsibility, you may wish to explain your reasons, that' fine, but DO NOT apologise.

You may encounter some surprise or resistance when you first start to say "no", especially from people who expect you to say "yes" based on your previous history of giving. However, it's unlikely that they will judge you for it, and if they do, that should confirm that you definitely made the right decision to say "no" as it's likely that the person is taking advantage of you.

Saying no when it isn't in your usual vocabulary can be a little daunting, however, the more you do it, the easier it becomes - it's like a muscle that gets stronger the more you use it. Therefore, wherever appropriate, start saying "no" today - remember the more you say it, the easier and guilt-free it will become.

3. *Stop comparing yourself to others*

If you're familiar with the 'Iceberg Model', you'll know that what you see from a person's actions and outward appearance is only a fraction of what's going on underneath. Whilst another person's life might look idyllic, we rarely know what's really going on.

We all have our own paths to follow and lessons to learn – by comparing ourselves to others, we're comparing ourselves to what we 'think' we see i.e. our perception (see Chapter 4) rather than what's really going on. Be your own person and focus on your own journey rather than what others are doing and your life will become far more fulfilling.

4. *Stop looking for permission/validation*

If you're always looking for permission from others before doing something, now is the time to stop. This is often a real problem for externally orientated people. Externally orientated people will look to others for advice, permission, and validation; they like to be told what to do rather than make their own decisions and they like to be told that their idea is a good one before they will take action. Internally orientated people on the other hand are much less likely to look to others for advice or guidance, but will look inside themselves for answers; they rarely require external permission or validation.

The problem with seeking permission, advice, or validation from others is that people will always have their own agenda.

They will give you advice based on *their* perception, filters, needs and wants which may be very different from your own. They may also have a conscious or subconscious need for you to be unsuccessful or not even try whatever it is that you want to do. I've met so many people who have not reached their full potential because 'someone else' didn't think whatever it is that they wanted to do, was a good idea or they told them that it was likely to fail and so they didn't even try. *You don't need anyone else's permission and you don't need anyone else's validation - YOU'RE ENOUGH.*

If you have the idea to do something, you already have everything you need within you to achieve it, otherwise you wouldn't have had the idea in the first place. You may need some support, money, training etc but you intrinsically have within you what it takes to achieve that goal.

Start tuning into your gut feeling - it's there as an internal guidance system that you should ignore at your peril. It's far more accurate than anything you could hear or learn externally. If you listen to your gut feeling, you'll rarely go wrong. Once you've decided what it is that you want, you then need to choose what actions to take and JFDI ('Just Flippin' Do It'!).

KEY QUESTIONS

Questions are such a critical part of our thought processes that we often underestimate their importance. Asking the right questions can mean the difference between staying in learnt helplessness and taking responsibility. *Whatever question we ask of ourselves, will always get an answer,* that's how our minds work. The problems tend to occur when we ask rubbish questions - ask rubbish questions and you'll get rubbish answers.

Questions can be disempowering, or empowering (in Chapter 6 we look at Victims versus Owners and how asking disempowering questions affects how we think and feel) in order to take control of your life, you need to start asking yourself empowering questions.

If there's something in your life that you'd like to change or a difficult situation that you're struggling with, instead of accepting it, ask yourself the following empowering questions:

- "What can I do to change this?"

- "What do I need to do to make this better?"

- "What else could this situation mean?"

- "What positives can I take out of this?"

- "What will I do differently as a result of this?"

37

- "Who can help me change this situation?"

- "Who can help me with this?"

- "What can I do to change this situation to a positive?"

When you take responsibility, you can see things more clearly and a completely new set of options open up. The great thing about taking responsibility is that *you* have the power to change almost anything you don't like and it doesn't have to be a long process, you just need to DECIDE and take consistent ACTION.

If you take action and things still don't change, it doesn't mean that you're a failure or that what you did wasn't good enough, it just means that the action you took wasn't the right action. Look at what you did, try something else, and if that doesn't work, try something else and keep trying until you find what does work.

The people who succeed and seem to be 'lucky' have usually simply taken more, prolonged action than 'unlucky' people/those who haven't succeeded. The more decisive you are and the more consistent action you take, the better the results you'll get.

CONTROL WHAT'S IN YOUR CONTROL

There are only three things in the entire world that you can control:

1. **Your thoughts**

2. The images you create in your mind

3. Your behaviour

Trying to control anyone or anything else is futile. You can't control the weather, traffic, other people, your health etc. In order for me to explain this in more detail, it's important to see how your thoughts, emotions and behaviour interact as a result of how you perceive a situation. The following diagram (Figure 1) is a good illustration of how one affects another and how they are inextricably linked:

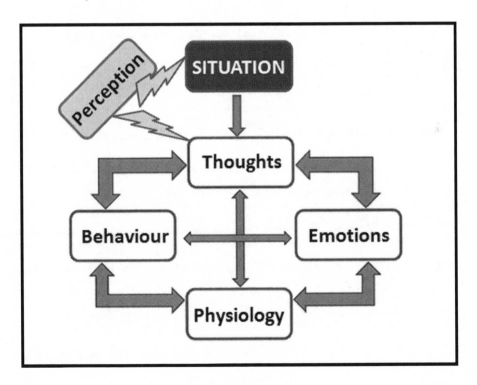

Figure 1

A situation occurs and your subconscious makes sense of it by running it through your filters (covered in Chapter 2) thoughts are then created which generate pictures in your mind (some people get specific feelings rather than clear pictures)

- Your thoughts and pictures directly affect your emotions (emotions can be positive, negative or neutral).

- Your emotions affect your physiology/body (body language, facial expressions etc - someone who is happy has very different body language to someone who's angry).

- Your physiology/body affects your behaviour (you act in a way that corresponds with the emotion you're experiencing i.e. happy, sad, angry).

- Your behaviour affects how you think and so the circle continues unless something happens to halt the loop effect or you consciously find a way to interrupt it.

This cycle is like a spiral, it can either be positive or negative e.g. have you ever started the day in a good mood but had one negative thought that attracted more and more until you ended up in a bad mood, ultimately shouting or being upset with yourself or the people around you? That's because you've actively put yourself into a negative loop or spiral through your thoughts, feelings and behaviours.

Once you're aware that this is what's happening, it can actually help you to STOP the negative thinking and therefore put a halt to the negative spiral effect. We'll talk more about how to do that later in Chapter 4.

THE PAST DOES NOT EQUAL THE FUTURE

One thing that I've learnt working with such a diverse range of clients is that *the past does not equal the future.* So many people believe that they can't do something or think that they can't influence their future because of something that happened in the past. They can also have this view if they received negative programming growing up e.g. watching what happened to parents, carers, friends and modelling their thoughts and behaviours. They then shutdown the possibility of achieving the life they really deserve without giving it their all.

Just because negative or 'unlucky' things have happened to you in the past or you've witnessed others not succeeding, it doesn't mean that it will happen to you. At any time, in any moment you can choose a different path, you can choose different thoughts, you can choose to do things differently, you can choose to make better decisions ... you can choose to try something new. We have so many choices, yet often we shut ourselves down through learnt helplessness.

You can break old patterns of behaviour and change your destiny in a second by simply *deciding to do something differently and taking action*; it could be doing one small thing that you've been putting off because you've been associating it with something negative from your past, or it could be as simple as saying "No". As I've said before, *one of the amazing things that life gives us is the opportunity to start again at any moment; the only thing that stops us is us!*

I truly believe that life is a series of choices and decisions and you make good ones and bad ones. The key is to keep trying - if something doesn't work, it doesn't mean that if you tackle it from another angle it won't work in the future. The most successful people try and try again until they achieve their desired results.

DON'T TAKE 'NO' FOR AN ANSWER

A great example of trying and trying until you succeed is one of the most well-known, Sylvester Stallone. He took his script for Rocky to hundreds of agents and film studios, only to be repeatedly rejected. Some people were downright rude about his script and even more derogatory when he suggested that he should play the lead.

Eventually, one studio said that they would take the script but wouldn't be casting 'Sly' in the lead role. He said it wasn't negotiable, if they took the script, then they took him too - the studio executives gave a resounding, "No". To cut a long story short, after constantly badgering them over a prolonged period, the studio relented, bought the script, and cast him as the lead and the rest, as they say, is history.

Bestselling authors, Jack Canfield and Mark Victor Hansen were rejected 140 times before landing a publishing deal for 'Chicken Soup for the Soul'; they have now sold over 125 million copies worldwide. JK Rowling landed a deal with Bloomsbury Publishing, after the daughter of one of their executives read a section of the book and demanded to read the rest. Before that, Joanna had been rejected by 12 other publishers. Her last four novels consecutively set records as the fastest-selling books in history, on both sides of the Atlantic, with combined sales of 450 million.

How many times have you stopped yourself from doing something because of a past experience? You tried something; it didn't work so you gave up. Most of the country's biggest entrepreneurs including Simon Cowell, Duncan Ballantyne, and Sir Richard Branson have openly admitted to failing on a grand scale at least once in their careers, but what makes them different is that they never stopped trying.

As an inventor, Edison made 1,000 unsuccessful attempts at inventing the light bulb. When a reporter asked, "How did it feel to fail 1,000 times?" Edison replied, "I didn't fail 1,000 times. The light bulb was an invention with 1,000 steps".

In each one of these examples, failure was not an option. Each achiever took stock, looked at the lessons they had learnt, what had and what hadn't worked, they made some necessary adjustments and tried again. *Their past did not equal their future*.

TRY, TRY AND TRY AGAIN

Is there something that you're not doing because you know someone else tried it and it didn't work for him or her? Or is there something that you tried in the past, but didn't manage to achieve? Well the other person isn't you and they don't have your unique skills and experience and I'm guessing that you failed not because you couldn't do it but because you stopped trying.

Work on shedding that old programming and those old views and take control of your life. What is it that you would love to do be or have but you've convinced yourself either you can't or that it won't work? Take a look at that 'something' with new eyes and stop making excuses, decide to take that first step, regularly evaluate your success and if something isn't working, try something else and keep trying until you succeed.

PERFECTIONISM AND FAILURE

I realise that if you're a perfectionist, trying something new without knowing what the outcome will be can be anxiety inducing. Many people never reach their full potential because they are perfectionists. I know people who either don't start or never finished their book, project, training, qualifications because they simply can't live up to their own exacting standards and therefore, either don't try, give up or stop trying, ending up feeling unfulfilled.

In fact, I've experienced some of that whilst writing this book. A book is something that could actually never be finished, there's always some new distinction to make or wording that can be altered. What I've had to do to combat my perfectionism is to choose a date and agree with myself not to add anymore or make any further changes after that date, which has been difficult to do, but a must if my book was ever to be published.

Nothing and no-one can ever be perfect. I heard a saying recently that I thought summed it up perfectly: *instead of striving for perfection, strive for excellence.* I love that because no one can be perfect, but everyone has the capacity to be excellent. Therefore, if you recognise yourself as a perfectionist, try reframing that view of yourself and work towards being excellent rather than perfect - it's much more realistic and will help move you out of learnt helplessness and into action.

YOU'VE BEEN PROGRAMMED

As I've mentioned previously, we make sense of the world around us by consistently reviewing the information we receive through our senses and interpreting it by running it through our filters. We develop our filters throughout our lifetime; however, they are largely influenced by our primary care-givers (mothers, fathers, grandparents, teachers etc) in our formative years. Initially we watch our care-givers' reactions and we subconsciously adopt their opinions and behaviours when we experience similar situations.

When we're young, we have no references, we're unknowingly being *programmed* by what we see, hear and feel going on around us, which we then display as our own 'learnt behaviours'. The problems begin when the people on whom we modelled ourselves have particularly negative or unhelpful programming themselves. I'm not blaming them here, they'll have been programmed themselves in much the same way - the same programming can go on for generations.

However, we do start to make our own decisions as we grow

up and experience new people and situations, which results in making new distinctions which in turn affect our filters.

OUR FILTERS

There are a number of aspects that make up our filters including our values, beliefs and rules which we largely learn through modelling. However, we also have our own inbuilt, internal filters:

- *Auditory, Visual, Kinesthetic* - How we process information through what we see, what we hear or what we feel - we all use all three but we do tend to have a preference.

- *Internally or externally focused* - Whether we look externally or internally for answers, validation, information etc.

By the age of six, we've learnt how to react to most situations. Whenever a new situation arises after that that age, our subconscious processing looks at how we react in similar situations and adopts that same response to the new situation.

The problem here is that unless you're consciously aware of your thoughts and behavioural responses and change them, you'll continue to react to circumstances in the same way that you did up to the age of six! Therefore, when you see someone with completely incomprehensible reactions or you find yourself reacting in a way that isn't appropriate and you can't figure out why, chances are you're simply re-running programming from your childhood.

An example of unhelpful reactions that is particularly common in women is to cry when they become frustrated (I've not yet seen this with any male clients, although it's certainly possible). I'd say that at least a quarter of my female clients suffer from this problem and I've found that it's particularly prevalent in senior women executives. They explain to me how they can't control their emotions when they become particularly angry or frustrated, they can't think clearly, feel overwhelmed and end up crying. They explain how embarrassing it can be and how they feel that their inability to be able to control it undermines their credibility - especially with their male colleagues.

There are usually two reasons why they do this:

1. *They learnt to do it by modelling their parents* - It doesn't necessarily mean that they modelled the behaviour from their female primary care-givers either. I had one client who told me that it was her father that used to cry a lot, not her mother.

2. *They receive some subconscious gain* (see Chapter 3, Secondary Gain) - When I ask clients what response they got to their crying when they were a child, they invariably tell me that they

were comforted and told it would all be OK - they were listened to and someone else dealt with their 'problem'.

However, as an adult, we're unlikely to get the same result we got as a child and therefore, it's necessary to change our reactions to something more appropriate.

CHANGING YOUR BEHAVIOURS

Often I find that simply knowing why you're doing something this is enough to facilitate a change. The subconscious mind will often make an instant change once it recognises that the old thoughts or behaviours no longer make sense. For those who need a little more help in changing old programming, there are some simple, easy-to-use techniques that I share later in the book. However, before I get into what those techniques are, it's important to understand Neural Pathways which are discussed at the beginning of the next chapter...

KEY LEARNING POINTS

1. TAKE RESPONSBILITILY

- Everything you have in your life right now is a result of what you've thought and the actions that you've taken.

- The only way to change what you don't like is to stop blaming others for how your life has turned out and take responsibility.

- If you don't like something in your life including how you're thinking and behaving - change it.

- In order to change, you need to DECIDE, make PLAN and take consistent ACTION, REVIEW progress and AMEND your plans as/when necessary.

2. CONTROL WHAT'S IN YOUR CONTROL

- Stop trying to control everything - you can't! You can only control your thoughts, your mental pictures and your behaviour.

- In order to halt a negative spiral, you have to change your thoughts to positive ones.

3. THE PAST DOES NOT EQUAL THE FUTURE

- Just because you may have failed at something in the past, doesn't mean that you'll fail again in the future.

- Just because someone you know or you've seen someone else fail doesn't mean that you will.

- The key to success is to NEVER GIVE UP and keep taking new/different action consistently.

4. YOU'BE BEEN PROGRAMMED

- You have learnt how to think and behave by modelling those around you.

- By the age of six you learnt how to react to most situations, for every situation that happens after that age, your subconscious searches your installed responses and chooses the most compatible or logical.

- Often the reactions we learnt as a child no longer serve us as adults and can lead to behavioural problems in adulthood.

CHAPTER 2

"We have an inbuilt need to remain consistent with our view of ourselves"

OUR FILTERS

As we've discussed previously, our filters are how we make sense of the world. We filter all the information that comes through our five senses in order to interpret what it means to us and what we should do about it. Some of our filters are 'in-built' i.e. we were born that way and others we learn by modelling our care-givers and later by incorporating learning and new distinctions from our life experiences.

- *Learnt filters*

  o Our values

- o Our beliefs

- o Our rules

- *In-built filters*

  - o Our learning style (whether we learn through what we see, what we hear or what we feel).

  - o Whether we filter externally or internally (whether we look outside or inside ourselves for answers and validation).

OUR VALUES

According to the Oxford English Dictionary, values are described as *'principles or standards of behaviour; one's judgement of what is important in life'*. Values are important and lasting beliefs or ideals that you have about what's good or bad and desirable or undesirable. Values have a major influence on your behaviour and attitude and in everyday-life you use your values as guidelines in all situations.

In Chapter 4, I'll talk in detail about how our view of the world is just our perception based on our filters - *a situation is just a situation until we put meaning to it.* How we see the world is a mish mash of ideas, views, expressions and learnt behaviours (programming) that we've gathered throughout our lives – it's the meaning attached to something that makes it real to us.

The values we learn by modelling are affected by our race, religion, country/region, the era in which we grow up in, etc. When we go to school, we adopt the values of our teachers and peers, when we leave school and carry on in education or enter the working world, we then often adopt a new set of values based on the companies we work for, our managers, our lecturers, our colleagues, our peers and our partners.

Our values, therefore, aren't set; they do change over time based on our exposure to different people, situations, practices and even TV. Television has had a huge impact on our Nation's values over the years. You only need to look at how sex, drugs, swearing were once completely taboo on TV and now they are the norm, which has contributed to a change in the values of a nation as a whole. The internet and social media also affects our changing values – nothing ever stays the same.

VALUES AND CONFLICT - WORK

Problems often arise when we have such strong values that we find it hard to be around people who don't share the same ones as us. I see this particularly in work situations where a client will tell me, "I hate my job, I need to leave". When I drill down into their reasons, it's rarely because they no longer like their job, but it's usually because their values don't (or no longer) fit with those of the company or their manager or the company/manager isn't congruent with their own values i.e. what they say and what they do are two different things.

There are two main options in this scenario:

1. Teach my client techniques that can help him/her learn to manage any conflict that may occur as a result of the difference in values.

2. Help my client identify their values and help them find another organisation that aligns more closely with them.

This situation is common following a company restructure where a new management team or new manager is appointed or where there is a business take-over; the new management having different values to the old, which often results in conflict. People generally resist change and if the new management team does things differently, there can be a perceived 'values' difference.

VALUES AND CONFLICT IN RELATIONSHIPS

Conflict can occur within personal relationships because of differing values; however, as we tend to surround ourselves with people who have the same or similar values to us, the values themselves are rarely the real problem. Where relationship issues tend to occur is when our rules surrounding our values are different (i.e. what has to happen to 'live' our values) we will discuss that later in this chapter.

Whilst it isn't likely that you would choose a partner who had radically different values to you (as you would find yourselves in constant conflict) it can be the case that your partner's values don't reflect those of his/her family. I often work with clients, especially in mixed race or mixed religion relationships, who experience values conflicts with their in-laws. This is a good example of where our values can change as we grow, at one point their partner may have had the same values as their family however, as a result of their life experiences, and they have undergone a shift in their values.

Values differences with in-laws can often be very trying, especially when the partner won't 'stand up' to his/her family. In these situations, I'll work with my client on managing their thoughts, changing the meaning of situations and generally teaching them coping techniques to help them deal with their in-laws more effectively. When we change our behaviour towards someone else, they *have* to change theirs in response (see Chapter 3 - 'You *can* change others' - for techniques that can help you if this is a particular problem for you).

IDENTIFYING YOUR KEY VALUES

When I ask clients (or delegates on my training programmes) what they consider their key values to be, I'm often greeted by blank stares. In my experience, very few of us actually stop to think about our values and yet they are one of the key drivers for our thoughts, emotions and behaviours.

There are many online tests that will help you pinpoint the values that are most important to you. However, this simple exercise that will help you quickly identify what your key values are and what matters to you most:

EXERCISE 1

IDENTIFY YOUR VALUES

Below is a list of common values. Look through the list and jot down three that resonate most closely with you, alternatively, you may have your own that are not on the list, if so, write those down. Once you have your list of three, rank them in descending order, one being the value you rate the highest.

NB: You'll probably identify with many of the values on this list, however, you should try to narrow it down to three - it doesn't mean that the other values aren't important, they simply aren't as

---

important as your top three.

VALUES LIST

ACHIEVEMENT ADVANCEMENT ADVENTURE AFFECTION ART AUTHORITY ACCOUNTABILITY ATTRACTIVENESS CHALLENGE CHANGE CLOSENESS CO – OPERATION CREATIVITY CARING COACHING COMPASSION COMMUNITY COMPETENCE CONNECTED COMPETITION CULTURE CONGRUENCE DECISIVENESS DESIGN DEMOCRACY EDUCATE EMPATHY FINANCIAL SECURITY EFFECTIVENESS ENERGISE ENCOURAGE ETHICS EXCELLENCE EXCITEMENT EXPERTISE FAME FINANCIAL GAIN FREEDOM FUN FRIENDSHIP GROWTH DEVELOPMENT FAMILY HELPING ALTRUISM SOCIETY HONESTY INDEPENDENCE INFLUENCE HARMONY INNER HARMONY IMPACT INVENTION INTEGRITY INTELLECT INVOLVEMENT TRANQUILLITY VENTURE LOVELINESS PEACE KNOWLEDGE LEARNING LOYALTY MONEY NATURE OPENNESS ORDER IMAGINATION STABILITY CONFORMITY PERSONAL DEVELOPMENT ORIGINALITY PLEASURE PASSION PLAY POWER PRIVACY PURITY QUALITY RECOGNITION RESPECT STATUS RELIGION GOD REPUTATION RESPONSIBILITY SECURITY SELF–RESPECT TRUTH WEALTH WORKING WITH OTHERS WORK LOVE PATRIOTISM RELATIONSHIPS WISDOM LEADERSHIP VARIETY RISK ENDEAVOUR EXHILARATION

YOUR TOP 3 VALUES:

1. _____

2. _____

3. _____

Keep hold of this list as we'll use it again later when we look at rules.

You may also want to do this exercise with your partner, especially if you've been experiencing any areas of conflict in your relationship. Knowing both of your top values, will help you to understand what drives you both and why situations (or your perception of situations) can sometimes be upsetting, confusing or conflicting. Simply having the ability to recognise where there are values conflicts can often help resolve them.

OUR BELIEFS

If a large proportion of the population can have the same values, how can there be so much conflict? It isn't actually the 'value' that is the problem, it's generally the beliefs and rules about what must happen in order for a value to be met that causes the problems.

As with values, our beliefs can change as we grow and age. For example, one of my clients told me that he grew up in a racist household with extreme racist views and beliefs; however, as he grew up and spent time with people outside his own race, he was able to make his own distinctions and develop his own belief systems, which was the exact opposite to his family. When we're born, we aren't born with any prejudices or beliefs; we're completely neutral towards all things.

Beliefs fall into two categories:

GLOBAL BELIEFS

These are beliefs that can apply to whole groups of people or things e.g. a particular profession, race, religion, sex etc. These beliefs tend to be very generic and we apply them to *everyone* in that group.

Some examples of global beliefs:

- 'People are...'

- 'Men are...'

- 'Women are...'

- 'Police are...'

- 'Christians are...'

- 'Immigrants are...'

- 'Black/white/brown people are...'

CORE BELIEFS

Core beliefs are the beliefs that we have about ourselves and our place in the world and again are formed as we grow up although not necessarily just through modelling, more importantly, how we've been treated growing up.

For example, I had a client recently who had to do a big presentation for an upcoming promotion interview at work. This was incredibly important to him and the job was almost guaranteed to be his as long as he didn't mess up the interview and presentation. However, he was terrified of having to stand up in front of others and told me quite categorically that he was 'stupid', and would be 'found out' as being such during the presentation.

When I dug a little into his past, I found that his father used to make him stand up in front of him and read aloud every night. If he made a mistake (which children often do, it's how they learn) he would shout at him and call him "stupid". Therefore, it isn't difficult to see where his fear of public speaking, coupled with his distorted view of himself as being 'stupid', came from.

I worked with my client using the techniques in Chapter 4 and taught him how to change his negative thoughts and how to manage his inner critic and I'm happy to say that he flew through the presentation and interview and got the promotion he deserved.

Core beliefs can be positive or negative and we can uncover ours by listening to the types of things we say:

LIMITING CORE BELIEFS

- "I'm always unlucky"
- "I never get things right"
- "'I'm always going to be unhappy"
- "I'm stupid/fat/a failure"

POSITIVE CORE BELIEFS

- "I always win"
- "I'm always successful"
- "I'm always a really lucky person"
- "I'll always be alright"

LIMITING CORE BELIEFS

Our core beliefs will always influence our thoughts, emotions and actions. They form the foundations of our personality and influence our interpretations of the world. For example, if you consider yourself to be unlucky, it's likely that you won't take responsibility for your life. You'll tend to blame others when things go wrong and it may even stop you from trying new things e.g. you'll likely tell yourself and others, "Why should I do that? I know it's not going to work out". Limiting core beliefs tend to become self-fulfilling prophecies.

Our limiting core beliefs are beliefs that we have about

ourselves that can shut us down both emotionally and physically and stop us from achieving the lives that we want and deserve. Identifying your limiting beliefs is important, because unless you know what they are and take steps to change them, you may become 'stuck' and then it will be difficult to move forward.

Core beliefs are like magnets, you'll always look (and usually find) evidence that backs them up and the more evidence you collect, the stronger the belief becomes. The down side of that is that you tend to repel anything that doesn't fit with your belief; this makes it hard to see or believe anything that would contradict or undermine them. *We have an inbuilt need to remain consistent with the way we view ourselves* and therefore we continually look for evidence to back it up.

Our limiting core beliefs aren't a true reflection of what's real. They are simply programmes or automatic thoughts (thoughts that we've had over and over again so that we now have them automatically in response to certain stimuli) that you can stop, if you choose to. After all, they are completely made up by you anyway.

OUR RULES

Our rules are how we 'carry out' our values and beliefs, it's what gives our values and beliefs meaning and this is often where the

64

real conflict occurs. To illustrate this, I had a client who wasn't getting along with his wife; they were having constant arguments, which he told me were becoming more and more upsetting. Not simply because of what they were arguing about, but because of *her* behaviour (according to my client). When I asked about their values, he told me that 'respect' was very high on both of their lists so he couldn't understand why she was so disrespectful to him when they argued.

I asked him what he meant by 'disrespectful' and he said that when he was growing up, to be respectful meant that you never argued. If there was any conflict, you would simply remove yourself from the situation until things calmed down. He said, "My wife is so disrespectful, she just wants to stand there and argue and I can't bear it, I have to walk away!"

I instantly thought that there was likely to be a 'rules' difference. I told him that as part of his homework he must ask his wife what her rules were around being respectful when she was growing up. In our next session, he told me that the 'respect rules' in his wife's family involved never walking away from a problem or argument, they worked through it until it was sorted, even if it meant raised voices and a certain amount of conflict resolution.

Both my client and his wife had the same value 'respect';

however, their rules around the value were very different. Once they had established that, they were able to come up with their own rules, rules that worked within their marriage and suited both of them. They actively made the decision not to continue the old patterns of behaviour inherited from their parents and created their own.

I know from my client that there have been subsequent times when the couple has both fallen back into their old patterns of behaviour, after all, they had been doing them most of their lives, and it did take a bit of practise to embed the new ones. However, they stuck with it and now have a far healthier way of resolving problems.

The next time you find yourself locking horns with someone and you just can't seem to break through, especially when you know that you have the same values, look at whether your rules are different. The good thing about rules is that you can change them easily once you know what they are. You don't have to continue with rules that have been programmed in to you if they no longer serve you; you can consciously make your own new ones. After all, they were never set in stone; it's likely that they have been passed down from generation to generation ... think of all the rules your family has around Christmas and weddings!

HOW MANY RULES DO YOU HAVE?

Have you ever noticed how many rules you have? Rules like:

- Family always comes first

- Never be late

- Children should always call their parents

- Never challenge a manager/someone in authority (this is a big one for the older generation – they tend not to challenge medical practitioners or anyone they perceive to be a higher social standing to themselves)

- Everyone *must* attend a family gathering

The more rules we have, the more chance there is of them being broken resulting in us experiencing some level of pain despite the fact that our rules are completely made up.

Here is a good example of a 'rule' that I picked up from my mum. She has always been very strict on timekeeping, which I seem to have 'inherited' or rather 'learnt' from her. It was drilled into me from an early age to *never* keep people waiting and to *always* be on time as being late is disrespectful. Therefore, one of my 'rules' is that I'll never be late for anything, unless there is a reason for it that is totally out of my control.

This often leads me to being ridiculously early for meetings; I'll often be an hour early rather than risking being 5 minutes late. In fact, if someone gets to a venue before me, I get quite upset about it and feel that I'm late. The downside to this, besides the amount of time I waste when I'm so early (although I do use the time to catch up on calls, emails etc), is that I expect everyone else to have the same rule as me, however, they rarely do.

Until I understood that we all have different 'rules' I'd get incredibly frustrated and agitated if someone was late. I'd see their lateness as a lack of respect toward me; however, now I know about 'rules', I've learnt to manage my own thoughts and emotions, causing me a lot less stress.

For another good example of rules, we need look no further than one of my good friends. She has five children all under the age of ten. I recently asked her how she manages to cope with having so many children all relatively young, her reply was, "Don't have too many rules."

She explained, "When the first two were born, we had all these rules about what they could and couldn't do or how they should and shouldn't behave. For example, "No eating in the living room" "No TV before bed" "Finish everything on your plate". The more children we had, the more impossible it was for our rules (and we had lots) to be met and I was feeling constantly disappointed, upset and out of control. Once we relaxed the rules, the easier things became and the happier the family is as a whole."

If you have too many rules, you're setting yourself up for a very painful life. There will doubtless be times when you'll end up breaking your own rules and they will definitely be broken by others. After all, most people won't even be aware of your rules as they'll have their own. Here is an exercise to help you establish what rules you're living by:

EXERCISE 2

IDENTIFY YOUR RULES

Taking the list of your top three values that you established during the earlier 'Values' exercise (Exercise 1), write a list of at least five rules that you have in order to 'live' each value:

Example:

VALUE 1 - RESPECT

Rule 1: Never be late

Rule 2: Never argue

Rule 3: Never raise your voice

Rule 4:   Always put others first before yourself

Rule 5:   Always be there when someone needs you

Now look take a critical look at your rules - do they all really work for you or are they unrealistic bearing in mind that others may not have the same rules as you? Using the example, *'Always put others before yourself'* it may be something that you tend to do, however:

- Is it likely that others will have the same rule and always put you first?

- Are you always able to put others first?

- Is it realistic to always put others first?

- Are putting others first to satisfy your own need on some level or theirs?

Once you really start to take a good look at your rules, you may find that some of them no longer make sense (maybe you've inherited them from your parents) and are simply leading you to experiencing unnecessary pain.

As rules are something that you learn or create, you can change them or let them go if they are no longer serving you or no longer make sense. Try loosening your rules for three days (see the next exercise) and observe what happens. It may be a little difficult to let go at first, however, you only have to try things and have positive results a couple of times before you'll start to subconsciously change your behaviour.

EXERCISE 3

LET GO OF YOUR RULES

For the next 3 days...

When someone or something upsets you, take a step back and establish if you're upset because one of your rules has been broken.

- If it is, which rule is it?

- Ask yourself if that rule is serving you or not.

- Ask yourself if that rule really matters or is it important/worth getting upset about it.

- If possible, ask the other person what their rules are around the thing that has upset you.

Often you'll find that people aren't deliberately going about trying to upset you. They're simply getting on with their own lives.

Once you discover the other person's rules, you may find that yours are actually out-dated and are no longer working for you.

If you find that you rules are out dated, either let them go, or change them for something more appropriate.

YOUR LEARNING STYLE

As we've mentioned earlier one of the internal ways in which we process or filter information is through our five senses:

1. **Visual (what we see)**

2. **Auditory (what we hear)**

3. **Kinesthetic (what we feel)**

4. Olfactory (what we smell)

5. Gustatory (what we taste)

We all have the ability to use all five styles; however, we tend to have a predominant one of the top three listed above. This is our preferred method (usually Visual, Auditory or Kinesthetic) for all our learning and communication. Once you know your preferred learning style, it enables you to understand your thoughts and feelings more and how they affect your behaviour.

It can also be helpful to identify another's predominant style, as it can massively enhance your communication and influencing skills with them. Much of the conflict we experience (in addition to values, beliefs and rules differences) can be attributed to a difference in learning styles; the likelihood is that the person you're in conflict with has a different one to you.

Let's look at learning styles in more detail:

VISUAL

People with a Visual preference process information through what they see. Visual people tend to care very much about their outward appearance and their houses/offices/workspaces etc tend to be very clean, neat and tidy ('a place for everything and everything in its place'). They tend to 'look' for evidence of what's going on rather than taking heed of what/how they're feeling or what they're hearing/being told.

It's relatively easy to identify a Visual person, based on their appearance and environment alone. However, the words they use are a good giveaway too. Visual people will say things like:

- "I *see* where you're going with this"

- "*Show* me how to do that"

- "Whichever way you *look* at it..."

Visual people tend to have visual skills such as painting, drawing, completing puzzles, they have a good sense of direction, make good writers, love reading, understand graphs and charts, are good at designing etc.

Visual preference people *look* for evidence to back up what they are thinking and for that reason I advise people who are going for interviews to take a folder in with them containing their interview preparation information. Not only does it help the candidate feel more at ease, but it also *shows* a 'Visual' interviewer that the candidate is well prepared; because they can *see* the candidate has done their preparation prior to the interview.

When learning something new, a Visual person will prefer to *see* someone doing it rather than hear how to do it or to have a go at doing it themselves straight away.

In a relationship setting, a Visual person generally wants their partner to take them places, they like to be shown off, have gifts bought for them or they want their partner to do things so that they can *see* that their partner loves them. Hearing that their partner loves them or receiving lots of physical attention (i.e. being hugged and kissed) is less likely to appeal to them. Of course, a Visual person may enjoy being hugged and told that they're loved, however, it's unlikely to mean too much to them if it isn't coupled with being *shown* that they are loved.

AUDITORY (HEARING)

A person with an Auditory preference will process information based on what they hear. They aren't overly concerned with what they see or how they feel, but it's what they *hear* that is important to them. In a business setting or college, Auditory people don't need to have lots of paper around them and they don't need to take many notes and pay little attention to what's being 'shown' on presentation screens or in reports/books. They tend to remember more of what they *hear* than what they see and feel. When learning something new, an Auditory person wants to *hear* how it's done rather than see it or try it for themselves initially.

Whilst it isn't as easy to spot an Auditory person by their appearance, here are the types of things that you're likely to hear them saying:

- "You're just not *listening* to me"

- "Can you *hear* what I'm saying?"

- "Let's *talk* about it"

- "That *sounds* good to me"

Auditory people tend think in words and have the following

types of skills: listening, speaking, storytelling, teaching, remembering information, arguing their point of view.

In a relationship, an Auditory person needs to hear, "I love you" and how much you care about them often and with sincerity. Showing them that you love them by buying them gifts or doing things for them or hugging and kissing them, whilst all very nice, will seldomly make them feel loved and appreciated unless it's accompanied with *hearing* that you love them ... and hearing it often.

KINESTHETIC

People with Kinesthetic tendencies, *feel* things and make judgments and decisions based on their feelings rather than what they see or hear. In a business setting, Kinesthetic people tend to go more on gut feeling - solid evidence and what they hear isn't so important as how they *feel* about something.

You can identify a Kinesthetic person not only by what they say, but they tend to be much more tactile then their Auditory and Visual counterparts. They tend to *feel* things quite deeply; they can be quite introspective and will look 'inside' to how they are feeling before making a decision. They tend to learn by actually *doing* the thing they are being taught rather than hearing about it or seeing it done by someone else. A Kinesthetic person will say things like:

- "I *feel* really cautious about this"

- "Let *me* try"

- "It's just a *feeling* I get"

- "If I'm *grasping* what you're telling me..."

Kinesthetic people tend to have skills in physical coordination, working with their hands, crafts, dancing, athletic ability, acting etc.

In a relationship scenario, Kinesthetic people need to *feel* loved. They need plenty of hugs, kisses, and physical attention. They love to be close to others and touch is very important. Hearing someone say they love them or someone buying them things or taking them places will mean little to them if they don't get the *feeling* of being loved through touch and physical attention.

HOW TO USE THIS INFORMATION TO YOUR ADVANTAGE

Once you're aware of learning styles, it has many applications in both your personal and work life. The following are some examples of where you can use preferred styles to your advantage in a work-based scenario. As we don't always know the learning styles of people in the situations I've listed, it's important that we cover all three in order to have maximum impact. By using all three, we have a better chance of being understood by everyone:

PRESENTATIONS

- *Visual* - 'Show' the pertinent points using visual aids e.g. handouts, props, screen presentation

- *Auditory* - 'Explain' your key points clearly and precisely using good paralinguistics (vary your tone, speed and pitch etc) to emphasise important points

- *Kinesthetic* - 'Use positive body language' and physiology, be expressive and open with your body language and facial expressions

INTERVIEWS

- *Visual* - 'Show' that you've done your preparation by bringing a folder with you containing two copies of your CV, typed questions that you want to ask the interviewer together with anything else you think is important - make sure that you're smartly dressed and well groomed.

- *Auditory* - 'Explain' your answers clearly and without waffling. A great way to prepare for an interview is to write down your key achievements from your current and previous roles and practise talking about them out loud. That way you can make sure that your answers are succinct and you don't waffle.

- *Kinesthetic* - Use appropriate body language and physiology. Make sure that your body language is open (don't cross your arms), keep good eye contact with everyone in the room (make sure that you also look at the person who may have their head down taking notes – they will still be able to *feel* your gaze even thought they aren't looking at you) smile, nod and use appropriate facial expressions.

TRAINING OTHERS

- *Visual* - 'Show' them how to do it, use props where possible (see presentations above). This type of person learns by watching someone else do it first, they also tend to take lots of notes and like comprehensive, well formatted handouts.

- *Auditory* - 'Explain' clearly exactly how to do what you're teaching them. This person learns by hearing how to do something, storytelling and using music is particularly helpful for Auditory learners.

- *Kinesthetic* - 'Let them have a go'. This person learns best by actually *doing* what you're teaching them, having a go themselves, as with Auditory people, Kinesthetic people also like to listen to music when studying as music affects their emotions.

If you're teaching just one person, find out their preferred style by asking pointed questions and listening for the clues in their response. See 'How to elicit learning styles' in the next section for some example questions that will help you extract both your own and other people's learning styles.

SALES ENVIRONMENTS

Knowing a customer's preference is critical in getting that elusive sale. I've used the example of car sales in order to demonstrate learning styles in a sales context:

- *Visual* - This person needs to 'see' themselves in the car and how they will look in it, they also like to have brochures that contain pictures and the car's statistics. Using their language you might say, "*Imagine* how you'll *look* in that new car"

- *Auditory* - This person needs to 'hear' about how the car performs and more importantly how the car sounds (they will be particularly interested in the stereo). Saying things like, "*Hear* the *sound* of that engine" "*Listen* to how amazing the stereo *sounds*" will appeal to an Auditory preference person

- *Kinesthetic* - This person needs to 'feel' the car, get them in it as quickly as possible and let them take it for a test drive -

You would say things like "Can you *feel* the softness of the leather and how *smooth* the car is when you drive it?"

By using the customer's own language, you're much more likely to secure the sale. Be careful not to mix the different preferences up e.g. if you said to a Visual person, "Feel the softness of the leather", whilst they will acknowledge that it does feel nice, it won't push them towards a sale. If in doubt as to what their style is, use all of them!

HOW TO ELICIT LEARNING STYLES

Eliciting a learning style is relatively easy if you ask the right questions and really listen for the answer. Remember that you're listening for the following types of words:

- Visual - *See, visualise, imagine, show, watch, look*

- Auditory - *Listen, talk, hear, tell, speak, discuss*

- Kinesthetic - *Feel, do, vibes, try, instinct, gut, move*

Ask them some simple questions and listen carefully to how they answer, looking out for the types of words mentioned above. Here are some example questions to use:

1. *When you get a new TV or Laptop do you:*

   a. Read the instructions first before you do anything? *(Visual)*

b.   Listen to an explanation from someone who has used it before? *(Auditory)*

c.   Have a go and work it out as you're doing it? *(Kinesthetic)*

2.   *When watching a presentation, do you take more notice of:*

a.   What the presenter says? *(Auditory)*

b.   What you see on a screen? *(Visual)*

c.   How you feel about the content and/or presenter? *(Kinesthetic)*

3.   *Do you feel more connected with people because of:*

a.   How they look? *(Visual)*

b.   What they say? *(Auditory)*

c.   How they make you feel? *(Kinesthetic)*

4.   *When you buy something new, what appeals to you the most:*

a.   How it looks or how you'll look in it? *(Visual)*

b.   How it sounds or what people might say about it? *(Auditory)*

c.   How it makes you feel? *(Kinesthetic)*

Another way to find out someone's style is to watch what they do:

- If they take lots of notes, like to look at things, have a very clean workspace, are always dressed and presented well, it's likely they are Visual.

- If they don't take very many notes, don't want to see brochures/information but want to listen to what you have to say, they'll be Auditory.

- If they want to have a go, touch and feel something, are more demonstrative and tend to sit/stand more closely to others, they are likely to be Kinesthetic.

Take some time out to understand the styles of the people around you at home or at work - start to really tune in and listen to how they talk, as they will unknowingly give you clues as to their learning style. The outcome will be that you'll begin to understand people better and relationships will become more harmonious.

COMBAT CONFLICT

Knowing this information comes into its own during conflict situations and can be especially beneficial within relationships. When you first start to date someone, you tend to display all styles to some extent, you tend to dress up and do things for your partner

(Visual), you tell them you love them or how great you think they are (Auditory), you hug and kiss them (Kinesthetic). However, over time, as you get used to being with each other, both of your preferred styles will come to the fore and you simply won't use as much of the other styles as you did when you first met.

This was apparent with a partner of mine. For some time we really weren't getting on and try as I might; I simply couldn't get him to understand my point of view. During one disagreement, I actually stopped when I heard myself saying, "You just can't *see* it, can you? I just don't understand why you just can't *see* what I'm saying", whilst my partner heatedly replied, "It's not that, it's that you're not *hearing* me! I'm telling you but you're not *listening!*"

It was at that point that I stopped and said, "That's the problem! We both have different learning styles - you're Auditory and I'm Visual!" He needed to *hear* how much I cared about him, whereas that isn't very important to me, I don't need to hear those words to know I'm loved, of course it is nice to hear every once in a while. However, I needed him to *show* me how much he loved me by doing things for me - not with massive gestures costing oodles money - but simply by *doing* things like making sure that he put the dishes in the dishwasher and put the rubbish out without me asking!

This was a real 'ah-ha' moment for both of us and we were able to track back through other disagreements and realise exactly what each other *really* meant by what we were saying and doing.

Think about times when you've experienced conflict either in your personal or work relationships. In retrospect, could it have been because your communication styles were different? Once you listen for the clues as to what a person's preferred style is, you can communicate with them using their style rather than your own, ensuring that they really understand your message, which will ultimately forge stronger relationships.

Clients who are in conflict with their teenage children find this information invaluable. Once they establish their child's preferred style, they can communicate in a way that the child actually understands and literally small miracles can occur.

KEY LEARNING POINTS

1. FILTERS

- Our filters are how we make sense of the world.

- Our filters are both inherent (we're born with them) and developed both by modelling others and through our life experiences.

- Our filters include:

  o Values/Beliefs/Rules

  o Learning style – Visual/Auditory/Kinesthetic

  o Whether we are internally or externally focused

2. VALUES

- Values are described in the English Oxford Dictionary as: *Principles or standards of behaviour; one's judgement of what's important in life.*

- We live our lives according to our values which are initially programmed in to us by our primary caregivers.

3. BELIEFS

- We have two types of beliefs, global (beliefs about groups of people or things) and core (beliefs about ourselves).

- As with our values, our beliefs initially come from our primary caregivers but can change as we grow and experience different things.

4. LIMITING CORE BELIEFS

- Our limiting core beliefs tend to be a product of both our early programming and from life experiences.

- Limiting core beliefs are a contributory factor for us not achieving the lives we want and deserve.

- Limiting core beliefs can be changed.

5. RULES

- We put rules to our values and beliefs in order to make them work.

- If we have too many rules or they are outdated, it will tend to cause us some level of pain or discomfort for ourselves and others.

- Our rules are often subconscious.

- We can have the same values as another person but different rules about how to live that value - that can often cause conflict.

6. YOUR LEARNING STYLE

- There are three predominant learning styles: Auditory (what we hear), Visual (what we see), Kinesthetic (how we feel).

- We all have a combination of all of three; however we tend to have a preference.

- Establishing another person's style can dramatically increase our communication and influencing skills as it allows us to deliver our message in a way that they will understand.

- Conflict often occurs where people have different styles as they will both literally be speaking different languages.

CHAPTER 3

"Always do what you've always done...
Always get what you've always got"

NEURAL PATHWAYS

I've heard *'You can't teach an old dog new tricks'* so many times, and it's one of those statements that really irritates me. More often than not, I think that people use it as an excuse for not trying something new, or they use it as a reason not to change something that they know they should. Everyone can change what they *think*, how they *feel* and how they *behave*; they just have to decide to and take a different course of action to what they have done previously i.e. *they need to build new neural pathways.*

In order for me to explain neural pathways (or in other words what goes on in your brain when you have a thought) in the simplest of terms, let's use the example of learning to drive. At first, when you start to drive, it's hard to co-ordinate everything; looking in the mirror, accelerating, breaking, using indicators etc and you have to be very vigilant and aware, consciously making sure that you do everything in the right order. The neural pathway that you create when you first start to drive will be very 'light', although you've learnt a bit; you still have to consciously think about what you're doing.

However, the more practise you do (and that's the key word, 'practise') the better you get and you slowly move from consciously driving (being very aware of what you're doing) to driving subconsciously. How many times have you driven somewhere and you can't even remember getting there, you drove there almost on autopilot? That's because the more driving practise you had, the deeper the neural pathway became and the actions required to drive, became ingrained in your subconscious, freeing up your conscious mind to think about other things.

AUTOMATIC THOUGHTS

Automatic thoughts are habitual and persistent, they repeat over and over, and the more they repeat, the more believable they seem, often setting off a whole chain of related thoughts that lead you to feeling worse and worse. This is because the more you have those thoughts, the deeper the neural pathway becomes so you're able to access them quickly and easily. These types of thoughts can be extremely destructive if you don't consciously notice and change them.

Unfortunately, there's no distinction between negativity and positivity as far as neural pathways are concerned. Whatever habitual thoughts you have (positive or negative) will create deep neural pathways, which then make that thought automatic. However, you can change your thoughts and behaviours; you just have to develop new neural pathways.

HOW TO CREATE NEW NEURAL PATHWAYS

You create new neural pathways by consciously choosing a different way of thinking and doing things. When you adopt the new thought/behaviour, the old neural pathway begins to lighten again as the new neural pathway deepens the more you use/do it. As a result, you move from the old way of thinking/behaviour to the new and from consciously thinking about the thought/behaviour to subconsciously doing it.

Clients often tell me that they are 'too old to change', which is actually a limiting core belief as we discussed in Chapter 2, as long as you 'think' that you can't change, it's very unlikely that you will. Of course, the neural pathways will be a little deeper in someone who has had a particular thought or behaviour for a long period; however, we all have exactly the same capacity to learn new things no matter what our age. The process is the same.

At first, noticing and changing your thoughts takes consistent practise, the hardest part is *noticing* when you're still thinking the old thoughts or displaying the same behaviours. However, you can train yourself to notice negative thoughts quickly and now that you've read this, you'll automatically be much more conscious of them. The key to making big changes is to STOP those negative thoughts as soon as you notice them and actively choose your thoughts and behaviours instead of being driven by your old programming. We'll talk more about how to do this in Chapter 4 where I explain some quick and easy techniques to use.

SECONDARY GAIN

Do you ever question why someone has a certain pattern of behaviour that makes absolutely no sense? On the other hand, do you sometimes wonder why you keep doing something that you know isn't right, but you keep doing it anyway? The answer is likely to be 'secondary gain' i.e. the subconscious benefit that we get from thinking and behaving in a certain way.

As we've already discussed, our reactions are largely programmed in to us as we grow, we've either watched and copied someone or we've learnt that by doing certain things or reacting in a particular way we get a desired outcome. That's where secondary gain comes in to play. For example, when you cried as a child, you may have received love and attention, so you did it again and again learning that crying produced love and attention, or you may have learnt that if you were quiet and didn't speak up, you would avoid being chastised so that's how you subconsciously chose to behave.

The problems begin when we're still running those old programmes into adulthood, e.g. if you were told growing up that 'children should be seen and not heard' and it was important to be quiet to avoid being reprimanded, in adulthood, you may find it difficult speaking up for yourself. Therefore, your secondary gain for being quiet as a child was that you weren't punished for talking or giving your point of view.

Secondary gain isn't always developed a result of programming growing up; it can develop in adulthood too. Take the example of a smoker: they know that smoking is bad for them and can cause all sorts of diseases and potentially death, so why do they do it? I often ask this question in workshops when I'm teaching secondary gain, there's always at least one smoker in the group who is happy to have their smoking habit questioned. Invariably when asked what their secondary gain is for smoking, they come up with some or all of the following benefits:

93

- "I get to take extra breaks in work."

- "It gives me a chance to take a breather away from chaos."

- "I get the chance to catch up on the gossip with other smokers."

- "I like the feeling of breathing deeply." *(You can do that anytime without the toxins!)*

- "It gives me something to do with my hands and it stops me eating."

Once you start to understand the secondary gain theory, it's much easier to see why we behave in the way that we do. It also allows you to have a good guess at why another person is behaving the way they are. Here are some examples that will explain secondary gain further:

FEELING	BEHAVIOUR	SECONDARY GAIN
Out of control	Aggressive	Control
Unheard	Confrontational	Attention
Frustrated		Authority
Undermined		

FEELING	BEHAVIOUR	SECONDARY GAIN
Unheard Overwhelmed Frustrated	Crying	Comfort Love Attention
Upset Overwhelmed Scared Anger	Avoidance	Avoid pain Keep safe

This is by no means an exhaustive list and feelings can create far more behaviours than I've written here, but I wanted to demonstrate how our emotions affect our behaviours and what our secondary gain may be for that behaviour. If you're honest with yourself, you'll be able to recognise what benefit you're getting from your thinking and behaviour. When I ask people what they think their secondary gain may be they usually say that they don't know, I then ask them either what their gut feeling is saying (your gut feeling is there for a very good reason and it's ALWAYS right) or "If you *did* know, what would you say the secondary gain is?"

Establishing a person's secondary gain, more than any other technique I use, creates the most 'ah-ha' moments – moments when a real shift in understanding occurs which allows the client to move on and make long-lasting changes. Once you recognise what the secondary gain is (for your behaviour or the other person's), you can change your response because you have a better understanding of why you or the other person may be behaving in a way that's upsetting or annoying etc.

When armed with that knowledge, it's likely that you'll become more understanding and compassionate towards yourself and others and that's when change can really start. When you come from a place of understanding rather than upset, you're in a much more resourceful state and able to make sound rational decisions.

Even the most difficult of relationships can be turned around as a result of understanding secondary gain, because once you react differently to someone rather than being on the defensive, they HAVE to act differently towards you, see 'You *can* change others' later in this Chapter.

ESTABLISHING ANOTHER PERSON'S SECONDARY GAIN

Looking at another person's secondary gain can be a useful tool, especially in a situation where you're in conflict with them. I had a new client referred to me by his company because he and another new manager had got to the point that their relationship was so poor that they were acting aggressively towards each other, literally going toe-to-toe on a daily basis. Not only was it making their working relationship untenable, but it also caused a strained working environment for everyone else in the office. My client's manager explained that even though my client had been with the company 30 years, his attitude and behaviour was unacceptable and unless the situation could be resolved, then they would be looking to 'remove' him from the business as *he* was seen as the problem.

When I had my first meeting with my client I asked him more about the 'new' manager. It transpired that although he was new to the company and to the industry, he had held a number of senior positions in other large, prestigious companies. When I asked what the problem was with the new manager at first he simply said, "We just don't get on!" He complained that the other manager was argumentative and wouldn't listen to him, he said, "I've been here 30 years, I know everything about this business so he *should* listen to me. He knows nothing about this industry and he keeps dismissing me like I'm an idiot!"

I asked my client the secondary gain question i.e. why his colleague may be behaving in that manner. After a lot of consideration and probing from me, he finally concluded that the other manager was probably feeling threatened by his knowledge of the industry and admitted that he had not helped him as much as he could have because of his defensiveness (a result of his own secondary gain). When I asked how *he* would feel if *he* was new into a company and someone was being defensive towards him, he replied, "I'd be devastated!" That was his 'ah-ha' moment.

Armed with his newfound knowledge, as soon as he got back to the office he arranged a meeting with his colleague where they managed to clear the air and he shared as much information as he could. Their relationship is now going from strength to strength, so much so, that they regularly have a beer together after work, something neither of them would have ever dreamt could happen. That's how quickly things can change when you look at secondary gain.

I must point out that I'm not suggesting that you tell the other person that you think you know what their secondary gain is (that would probably make matters worse), but it's useful for you establish what it might be, as it will allow you to view a situation/person differently and help change your perception. Clients often say, "But how can I be sure that I've got someone else's secondary gain right?" well you can't, but if your gut feeling is telling you it's right, then it probably is and that's enough for you to try a different approach at the very least.

Remember that *people are always just doing the best for themselves and their behaviour is very rarely personal* (although it's difficult to see that sometimes). Once you understand that, however, it's much easier to change your approach and achieve better results.

YOU CAN CHANGE OTHERS

...But only if you change yourself first!

I often hear, "You can't change others but you can change yourself". Technically you can't change others, however, once you change yourself (your thoughts and behaviours) the other person *has* to change in response - it's an automatic process which occurs in the subconscious. Changing your behaviour to influence another's is easier when you can make an educated guess at either your own or the other party's 'secondary gain'.

As I described in the 'new versus old manager' example, work-based conflict is a common problem that I often work with clients to resolve. Conflict in work not only affects work performance, but as both our work and home lives are intrinsically linked, it stands to reason that if we're having problems in work, we often take them home with us. Sometimes this conflict can get to the point where it affects every aspect of our lives and a client will say, "I have to leave, I just can't work with that person anymore. I'm so unhappy and it's affecting my family". I'll then work with them to change the way they think and feel about that person before taking the drastic step of looking for a new job.

Firstly, I'll look for any secondary gains evident on either side. The next stage is to work with the client to change how they actually visualise or picture that person in their mind's eye. Once you change the picture of a person, it's very difficult to see them in the same way again.

Occasionally I'll have a client who says that they can't visualise - quite often, those people also report not being able to dream. We all visualise, it's just that some people can visualise more clearly than others can. Some people get more of a feeling and with others, their internal narrative is stronger (remember Visual/Auditory/ Kinesthetic that we talked about in Chapter 2). What we've been told growing up can also have an effect on what we visualise, often people who have been told that they have 'no imagination', find it hard to visualise which reinforces what others have said to them, becoming a self-fulfilling prophecy.

Even if you struggle visualising, I suggest that you try the following exercise. Like anything, your visualisation skills will get stronger the more you use them and they can be very powerful - see Chapter 5 for information on the power of visualisation.

EXERCISE 4

HOW TO FEEL DIFFERENTLY ABOUT ANOTHER PERSON

Read this exercise at least once before you try it. It's better to do it with your eyes closed, but if that's not possible, then open is fine:

1. Have a picture in your mind of the person you want to feel differently about.

2. Make that picture clear and bright and colourful, feel the feelings that you associate with them and clearly hear how they talk.

   Some people actually have a video of the person they dislike that they run repeatedly, or they will often say that they can see that person walking towards them and it brings up strong emotions, if that's the case with you and then run that video.

3. Whilst you have that picture/video clearly in your mind, change something about the person; give them Mickey Mouse ears, Ronald McDonald hair, add some sort of 'appendage', change the sound and tone of their voice and add some funny music (circus music works well for this)

4. If you're running a video, have that person sit on a clown's tricycle as they come towards you or have them walk differently

(remember Monty Python's 'Ministry of Silly Walks'?). Simply change something about them that makes you laugh or smile when you think about it - anything that makes you see them differently in a non-threatening way.

5. Keep that picture in your mind for a few seconds and make it bigger, brighter, and more colourful, make the sounds louder and feel how that person now makes you feel as you see them in your mind's eye in their 'altered' state.

   If you're seeing a video, run it a few times from beginning to end until it's very easy to see it clearly and you can return to it whenever you want to. See what you see, feel what you feel and hear what you hear and amplify all aspects as much as possible.

   Keep practising, seeing that new picture or video often over the next 24 hours and really experience how differently you now feel and think about that person.

I must do this exercise at least twice a week with different clients. I had one Board Director who was in constant conflict with the CEO of his organisation. He said that every time he saw the CEO walking towards his office, he would automatically go into defensive mode and he could feel himself becoming agitated and aggressive.

When I did this exercise with him, he told me that he had chosen to see the CEO coming towards his desk on a clown's tricycle and with Ronald McDonald hair, which really made him chuckle. After running this 'video' a number of times with the addition of 'circus music', my client found it difficult to see his CEO with his normal appearance.

Once back at work, when the CEO came towards him, he automatically visualised the tricycle and found that he was unable to access his old, hostile feelings. My client told me that once he started to see the CEO differently, he no longer had the old negative feelings towards him, which allowed him to deal with him in a more effective way. Once his attitude and behaviour changed towards the CEO, then the CEO's behaviour automatically changed towards him, creating better communication between them and an enhanced relationship ensued.

IT'S NOT MANIPULATION, ITS INFLUENCING!

Occasionally, I'll get clients who say, "Isn't changing your behaviour like that manipulative?" or "I'm not changing and giving into them, I'm not prepared to let them win!" My reply, "It's not manipulative and you're not giving in, it's called INFLUENCING - getting the result you want, which I'm assuming is to make your relationship easier, giving you more control so that you don't need to leave your job!"

As I've said previously, if you change something about yourself and it results in you acting differently towards someone, then the other person *has* to act differently towards you - it's how it works. At first, the other person may not necessarily notice a change at a conscious level and they won't be able to pinpoint exactly what the change is, they will simply know that you're acting differently towards them and therefore, they will automatically act differently towards you.

In summary, the old adage, 'You can't change others but you can change yourself' isn't strictly true. I prefer, *'You* CAN *change others, if you change yourself first'*.

ALWAYS DO WHAT YOU'VE ALWAYS DONE...

... always get what you've always got

According to Einstein, the definition of insanity is, *"Doing the same thing over and over again and expecting a different result"*. If you continue to do the same things repeatedly, you absolutely can't realistically expect a different outcome, yet so many people do. Many of my clients will complain about their situation or about another person and I'll ask, "What have you done differently? What have you changed?" and the answer invariably is, "Nothing!"

If you're in a stale relationship that isn't growing or moving forward, if you hate your job and it never gets any better, if you hate your financial situation and can't see an end to it, if your kids are constantly driving you crazy, if you have people in your life that you keep moaning about ... DO SOMETHING ABOUT IT!

Whatever you're experiencing in your life, you have the ability and power to change it. Take responsibility and stop waiting for an outside intervention or falling into the trap of, "It'll get better when..." It will not get better until you DECIDE to make it better and take ACTION to change it.

I had one client who during every session would complain about his partner and how she was a stay at home mum but she wouldn't clean the house. I could see that it was clearly upsetting him, so asked what he had done about it. He said, "I keep telling her she HAS to clean the house." I said, "But you've been having that conversation with her for months, haven't you?" He replied, "Yes - and she's still not doing it!"

I pointed out that it was unlikely that she would change and start cleaning and asked him what else he could do about it. He concluded that he could either do it himself (which he absolutely refused to do as he was working long hours and simply didn't have the time) or get a cleaner. The money to pay for a cleaner wasn't an issue; it was the *principle* that was a problem for him. He thought that his wife *should* do it because she was a 'stay at home mum'.

I said, "But she isn't doing it, so you either come to terms with the fact that you live in a messy house or *you* clean it or you get a cleaner." I told him that he could continue to get upset and it could ultimately ruin their relationship (or at the very least make them both dreadfully unhappy) or he could get a cleaner and move on. After some deliberation, he got the cleaner!

Often you only need to make one small change, one small decision that will set a course in motion. Whatever it is that's not right in your life, don't keep complaining about it, do something about it, take responsibility. Make one small shift in your thinking or decide on one action you can take to change things and see what happens. So often we find ourselves in 'learnt helplessness' i.e. we think we're powerless to change our situation. The truth of the matter is, there is always *something* you can do, you just have to try and if that thing doesn't work, then try something else and keep trying until you find something that does work.

THE POWER OF INTENTION

Unfortunately, it's incredibly easy to float through life not actually achieving anything. One way to combat that and to ensure that whatever you spend your time doing is worthwhile and moves you forward, is to set your intention, no matter how big or small the activity. Be clear about your outcome for every situation and you'll find your life much more fulfilling, for example:

- If you're having a meeting, decide on your desired outcome. How many meetings have you attended where at the end you thought, "What was all that about? What a waste of time!"

- If you're going to your friend's house, what outcome do you want? Is it just to hang, to laugh, to make them feel good? If you set your intention on the way there, you are much more likely to enjoy your time

- If you're having any kind of conversation, think about the outcome you want

- If you send an email, what's your intention? Are you looking for an output, the other person to do something or just to pass on information? Be clear on what you're asking for and your expectations

SETTING GOALS – USE INTENTION

If you're goal setting, don't just write the goal, but be clear about *why* you want it, *why* it's important to you, *how* it will change your life or how you'll feel when you achieve it. Once you set a clear intention for your goal, you'll move towards its completion much more quickly. It's the reasons *why* we want something that moves us towards it, not simply just wanting the goal in itself.

Being clear about why you're doing something will help you to question your motives and stop you from wasting time, money and resources doing things that aren't necessary, that don't serve you or that you don't really want. When I decided to write this book, someone said to me, "That's a lot of work, why would you want to do that?" It got me thinking about my intentions and I decided to write them down (another good piece of advice is, *what gets written down gets done* – you're far more likely to achieve something that you've written down). Here are my intentions for writing this book:

- To help as many people as possible achieve better lives through learning and applying techniques that I describe in the book

- To give to my clients as a summary of the work we've done together in face-to-face sessions, so they don't have to remember everything afterwards and have something to refer back to in between sessions and after the coaching relationship ends

- To assist my standing as an authority in my area of expertise

- To provide prospective clients with a taste of what they can expect from my coaching

- To use as a marketing tool

Being clear about what it is that you want from a person, situation or task will save time and energy and help you get what you want more quickly.

KEY LEARNING POINTS

1. NEURAL PATHWAYS

- Neural pathways in our brains get stronger the more times that we do something.

- If we've had the same thought over and over again, it becomes automatic and the neural pathway for it becomes deep.

- We can change our thoughts and behaviours by *choosing* to think or do something in a new or different way.

- When we start to do something in a new or different way, we create new neural pathways. The more times we practise the new way, the deeper the new neural pathway becomes and the new action or thought will become automatic.

2. SECONDARY GAIN

- Secondary gain is the subconscious benefit that we get from thinking and behaving in a certain way.

- We can usually have a good guess at another person's secondary gain which allows us to adjust our behaviour towards them.

- The secondary gain we get from doing, thinking or saying

something isn't always as a result of childhood programming, it can also develop in adulthood too e.g. smoking.

3. YOU CAN CHANGE OTHERS

- We can change others but only if we change ourselves first.

- Once we make changes to our thoughts and behaviours, others will automatically react differently towards us.

- If you're in conflict with another person and you want to change how you feel about them, change something about their appearance when you visualise them (the funnier, the better).

- Practise visualising that 'new' person repeatedly and you'll notice a change in how you feel about them which will affect how you behave towards them.

4. ALWAYS DO WHAT YOU'VE ALWAYS DONE...

- ... Always get what you've always got.

- You can't keep doing the same thing and expect a different result.

- If you want something or someone else to change, *you* have to change something about yourself first.

- If you aren't prepared to change or do something differently, then the situation is unlikely to change.

5. SET YOUR INTENTION

- If you set your intention for everything you do, you'll achieve far more.

- Having strong reasons as to why you want to achieve a goal will get you much further than just establishing a goal without intention.

CHAPTER 4

"Change your thoughts...
Change your world"

THOUGHTS BECOME THINGS

As we've seen in earlier chapters, our thoughts influence everything, because they affect how we feel, our physiology and our behaviour. Therefore, having control of our thoughts is a key skill that that can be easily learnt and once mastered, will continue to change your life in a positive way forever.

THE VITAL STATISTICS

According to The National Science Foundation, we have anything between 50,000 and 70,000 thoughts per day depending on how deep a thinker we are. Other sources estimate that we can have up to 100,000 thoughts per day. Interestingly, some researchers believe that 95% of the thoughts that we have every day are the same as the ones we had the day before - **95%!**

That statistic certainly explains why, if you're a consistently negative thinker, it can be difficult to get yourself out of that downward spiral. If you think negatively up to 100,000 times a day and we know that your thoughts affect your emotions and behaviours, then that explains why you might be living an unhappy life. You'll be living in one great ball of negativity and the neural pathways will be very deep.

WHERE DO OUR THOUGHTS COME FROM?

Have you ever thought about where your thoughts come from? When I ask this question normal reactions range from staring at me blankly, some people shrug, some look uncomfortable, others look completely perplexed, like I've asked them to solve the mysteries of the universe. Very occasionally someone may tentatively ask, "Me?"

Bingo! Yes, your thoughts come directly from YOU. You create them based on your values, filters, rules, programming and learnt behaviours. Nobody *gives* you your thoughts, they aren't placed there by some mystical force; you create them in their entirety.

THIS IS FANTASTIC NEWS because if you have repetitive, negative thoughts it means that you can change them! Being able to control your thoughts gives you control over every situation, it enables you to make better decisions based on what's really going on rather than your negative interpretation, which isn't reality.

This is another of the most transformational changes "ah ha" moments I see in my clients; when they realise that they have control over their thoughts and they can change the ones that aren't working for them. For some, it's like a revelation, it's so simple and yet we aren't ever taught it. I believe it's something we should be teaching our children and should definitely be taught in schools. The world would be a much happier place if we all knew and understood that our thoughts are generated by us and therefore, are within our power to change. Once you realise that you can control your thoughts, you can change everything...

YOU CAN'T HAVE TWO THOUGHTS AT ONCE

You can't have two thoughts at the same time, it's impossible therefore, the minute you notice yourself having a negative thought (and now you've read this, you'll start to notice them more often), simply change it to something that makes you feel good. Think about lying on a beach or picture someone you love or something you love to do, change the picture to anything that makes you feel happy. The minute you do that, then the focus will automatically shift from negative to positive and will stop your negative thoughts spiralling out of control.

Unfortunately, once you have one negative thought (even if you're in a relatively good mood to begin with), if you don't notice and change it to a positive one, it will attract more, left unchecked, one small negative thought can spiral into a full blown negative attack. *Like attracts like*, it is basic law of attraction, ***what you think about you get more of.*** Therefore, it's really important to STOP negative thoughts as soon as you realise that you're having them.

HOW TO CHANGE YOUR NEGATIVE THOUGHTS

Let me be clear, I'm not simply advocating 'positive thinking' here, the problem with thinking positively is that you have to think about it and to do that on a consistent basis is difficult and you're likely to fail and give up after a short time. However, the more you start to notice your negative thoughts and change them quickly; you'll start to notice a significant change in your thinking patterns as start to create new neural pathways. The following exercise is a great way to help you gain control of your thinking:

EXERCISE 7

CHANGE YOUR NEGATIVE THOUGHTS - VISUALISE

Read the whole exercise at least once before you try it. Make sure you're in a comfortable place, you can do this exercise with your eyes open or closed, however, closed would be more beneficial and I suggest for the first few times you do it, do it somewhere quiet where you won't be interrupted.

1. Vividly imagine something that makes you happy (e.g. your partner, your children, a beautiful sunset, lying on a sun-soaked beach).

2. Make that picture big - you might want to project it up onto the side of a skyscraper!

3. Give it vivid colour.

4. Make it into a movie.

5. Give it a loud sound track.

6. Vividly feel how you would feel if that image/video were real, see what you would see and hear what you would hear.

7. Keep repeating your picture or video until you can instantly access it whenever you think of it.

8. As soon as you notice a negative thought, immediately change the picture to your happy one and you'll notice that the negative thought will disappear almost instantly.

9. If the negative thought comes back or as soon as you notice another negative thought, immediately swap to your happy picture/video.

It's very easy to do, yet very powerful. The more you practise this visualisation technique, then the easier it will be to access your happy thought/video (you'll create a deep neural pathway making the new thought easy to access). I advise my clients to do this exercise for at least 5 minutes a day, preferably as part of their bedtime routine.

The following is another exercise that's just as effective in stopping your negative thoughts; however, it isn't quite as pleasant as the previous one!

EXERCISE 8

CHANGE YOUR NEGATIVE THOUGHTS - ELASTIC BAND

Keep an elastic band on your wrist and as soon as you notice a negative thought, snap the elastic band so that it reminds you to STOP the thought!

Please note that it shouldn't hurt! It should just be a reminder to stop the thought pattern before it attracts similar negative thoughts. The more you do this, the more quickly you'll train your brain to notice and change negative thoughts quickly and it will become a habit without needing the band.

EXERCISE 9

CHANGE YOUR NEGATIVE THOUGHTS - JUST SHOUT "STOP"

This is my favourite 'negative thought stopping technique' and it's the one I use most often to halt my own negative thoughts.

- When you notice a negative thought, simply shout "STOP" and literally visualise moving the thought on.

If I'm in the car, I'll bang the steering wheel or if I'm not

JO BANKS

> driving I might clap my hands or stamp my foot (if no-one else is around of course!)
>
> It's another simple but affective technique for stopping those negative thoughts.

All three of these exercises are what we call in NLP terms, pattern interrupts. The more you interrupt your usual pattern, the harder it will be for you to keep doing it. Think of a DVD or CD, once it's scratched, it simply won't play the same again. Our thoughts work in much the same way. The more we interrupt our negative thought patterns and replace them with something better, the harder it will be to access them and after a while, they will disappear almost completely as you'll build new, stronger neural pathways to replace the old ones.

FIND YOUR 'SAFE PLACE'

I use a version of Exercise 7, with clients who are suffering high levels of stress or anxiety. I ask them to visualise somewhere that they feel safe, loved and in control. Once they have vividly imagined this place over and over, I tell them to go to this 'safe place' in their minds whenever they experience negative emotions. Having somewhere where they can escape to even if it isn't real

120

(remember, *the mind can't tell the difference between something real and something vividly imagined*) gives them the opportunity to calm down, to take control over their thoughts and emotions and as a result, they are able to think more objectively enabling them to be more resourceful.

THE NEGATIVITY DIET

If you're a highly negative person, it can be difficult to realise just how negative you are because your negativity is normal for you. However, if you aren't consciously aware of what you're doing or thinking, how can you change? The following exercise will help you to recognise your negative patterns of thinking.

EXERCISE 10

THE NEGATIVITY DIET

Over the next three days, make a conscious decision to notice any negative thoughts you may have and change them quickly to your 'happy thought' from Exercise 7.

If you don't notice your negative thoughts immediately and you end up in a negative spiral, you have to start the three days again.

It's likely that the initial three days will turn it to at least ten!

> The point is to get you into the *habit* of noticing your negative thoughts and changing them. The more you practise the more sustained your positivity will become.

RECURRING THOUGHTS

Occasionally, there may be a very good reason for a negative thought, especially if it's a recurring one. If a thought keeps coming back, check to see if there's a message in it. Is there something that you need to do, or some lesson you need to learn or heed? If there is, deal with it and take some action as soon as you can. Thoughts with a message or an action will keep coming back until you do something about them. Once you've taken action, you'll usually find that the repetitive thought will disappear.

If a recurring thought doesn't have a message, it's likely that it's another automatic thought as we've discussed previously. The thought's neural pathway is likely to be deep and therefore it comes to you quickly and easily. A good way to deal with those thoughts is to acknowledge them and literally wave them on. Look up, acknowledge the thought, take your hand and literally swipe it away. You may even want to add a bit of commentary such as, "Go away, I don't have time for you right now!" It sounds a little crazy and far too simple to be effective, but it works.

Using any of the 'change your thoughts' techniques I've described will help you to gain control over your negative thinking. The more you apply these techniques, the quicker you'll deepen your new neural pathways and you'll eventually stop having the old repetitive automatic thoughts. It would be unrealistic of me if I said that you would never have a negative thought again, of course you will, but my aim is to give you options and techniques to control them when they do come.

UNHELPFUL THINKING PATTERNS

We've covered negative programming in detail throughout the book, but we haven't really looked at the unhelpful thinking styles that negative programming can produce. In psychology, these types of negative thought patterns are described as cognitive distortions; ways that your mind convinces you of something that is or isn't true. These distortions reinforce negative thinking, confirming that what we're thinking is rational and accurate.

Distorted thinking adds to the negative spiral effect. As we know our thoughts affect our emotions, affecting our physiology and behaviour. That then triggers our next thought and that's how we find ourselves in a downward spiral - our thoughts attract more of the same types of thoughts – *like attracts like*.

The following are 10 common unhelpful thinking patterns,

which once you understand them, can make it easier to identify your distorted thinking, giving you the opportunity to change your thoughts to ones that are accurate and that work for you, breaking your old programming and negative thinking:

DISTORTION	EXPLANATION
All or Nothing Thinking	This is often referred to as 'black or white' thinking - a situation or person is either good or bad, right or wrong, success or failure, any shades of grey are discounted. • "Every time I do something I mess it up" • "I never get things right" • "I always get stuff wrong"
Over-Generalising	Seeing a single unpleasant or negative incident as evidence that *everything* is unpleasant or negative, or that everything you do in the future will go wrong. • "I can't believe that I failed so badly, nothing will ever go right for me" • "I didn't get an interview - I'm never going to

DISTORTION	EXPLANATION
	get a job" • "That date was awful, I'm not trying to go on anymore"
Mental Filter	Only paying attention to certain types of (usually negative) evidence that 'fit' your view of the world, ignoring chunks of evidence (usually positive) that may provide an alternative view: • "That doesn't count." • "You hate all the work I've done." • "There's no point trying, everything went wrong last time."
Disqualifying the Positive	Discounting anything positive that has happened, that has been said to you or that you have done: • "They said they liked my work - they didn't mean it." • "She said my dress was pretty, I wonder what she wants."

DISTORTION	EXPLANATION
	• "They said my presentation was great - they were just being nice to me."

Jumping to Conclusions	Making a negative interpretation or prediction about something even when there's no evidence to support it, there are two key types:
	
	1. *Mind reading* - imagining what others are thinking/saying about you:
	
	   • "I just know they don't like me."
	
	   • "I know they're trying to sabotage my efforts."
	
	2. *Fortune telling* - thinking that you know what is going to happen in the future:
	
	   • "I just know it's not going to end well."
	
	   • "There's no point trying ... it won't work."

Catastrophising (Magnifying & Minimising)	Thinking that something is better or worse than it really is - blowing negative things out of proportion and downplaying positives : • "I made a mistake with that report - they're

DISTORTION	EXPLANATION
	going to fire me." (Magnifying) • "They said what I'd done was brilliant, but it really wasn't." (Minimising)
Emotional Reasoning	Assuming feelings reflect fact, regardless of the evidence or lack of evidence. Feeling something and thinking that it must be true, which often leads to self-fulfilling prophecies i.e. believing what you feel, and behaving in a way that reflects the belief: • "I feel really embarrassed, so I must be stupid." • "I feel ugly, so I must be ugly." • "I feel useless, so I must be useless."
Using 'Should' 'Must' 'Ought'	Having rigid views of how you and others 'must' 'should' and 'ought' to be. This often leads to feeling negative emotions such as disappointment, anger, frustration, guilt and resentment:

DISTORTION	EXPLANATION
	• "I *should* do this." • "They *ought* to be doing that." • "I *must* get that done."
Labelling	An extreme form of 'all or nothing' thinking and over-generalisation, rather than describing a specific behaviour, assigning a negative and highly emotive label to ourselves or others that will rarely change even if there is evidence to the contrary: • "I'm so stupid." • "They're an idiot." • "I'm completely useless."
Personalisation	Automatically assuming responsibility and blame for negative events that aren't under your control. You may also tend to take general feedback to heart: • "It's my fault my dog is sick, I left him with someone else."

DISTORTION	EXPLANATION
	• "It's their fault. I had nothing to do with it." • "The feedback my boss gave me on that report made me feel sick."

Go to www.thoughtsbecomethings.co.uk and sign up to receive a copy of this list.

It's important to understand when and where you may be having thoughts that are unhelpful or distorted. Once you recognise the patterns of unhelpful thinking that you use most often, you can examine those thoughts and find more positive and realistic ones as replacements. By knowing what triggers them i.e. where you are or what you're doing when you have them, you can spot patterns. When you're armed with that knowledge, you can change your thoughts more quickly as you know what's likely to trigger them before it happens.

When you read the list above there's a good chance that you'll notice unhelpful patterns of thinking that you'd like to change. If that's the case, use the following exercise to identify the thought, how you're distorting it and find a more realistic thought to replace it. Once you recognise that your thoughts are not necessarily true, it makes it much easier to change. As I've said previously, when something no longer makes sense to us, our subconscious will usually automatically make the changes necessary to adopt a new thinking pattern/ behaviour that does make sense.

EXERCISE 11

CHANGING DISTORTED THINKING PATTERNS

Use this exercise as many times as necessary to start to clear up your negative, distorted thoughts and replace them with ones that are more realistic.

1. What is the negative thought you're having?

_____

_____

2. Which of the unhelpful thought patterns/distortions (from the list above) are you applying to that thought?

_____

3. What evidence do you have to support the thought?

_____

_____

_____

_____

4. What evidence do you have that doesn't support the thought?

_____

_____

_____

_____

5. What is a more realistic thought?

_____

_____

_____

Visit the website at www.thoughtsbecomethings.co.uk to access free worksheets that will help you keep track of distorted thinking patterns. Keep a sheet with you during the day so that you can record any thoughts that come up. If you regularly review your unhelpful thinking patterns, you will be able to identify any triggers and patterns, enabling you to take action to deal with things in a more positive way before they even happen. Clients often tell me that once they start to do this, they start to pinpoint exactly when they are about to have a negative thought or behaviour and are able to stop it or change something before it takes a hold.

THE POWER OF PERCEPTION

As we've discussed in previous chapters, each one of us perceives a situation in a different way based on how we filter information and how we see the world. A situation is just that, a situation and nothing more, it has no meaning, it isn't good or bad, it's entirely neutral, it only becomes something when we put a meaning to it. That meaning is based on numerous factors including our ethnicity, religion or the other person's ethnicity, religion, our current mood, what's happened to us that day, together with our previous experience of a similar situation, our learnt behaviours, our general view of the world etc and is usually made at a subconscious level.

Looking at the Figure 2, the diagram we discussed in Chapter 1, it's our perception of a situation that affects our emotions, that changes our physiology and affects our behaviour; it isn't actually the situation itself.

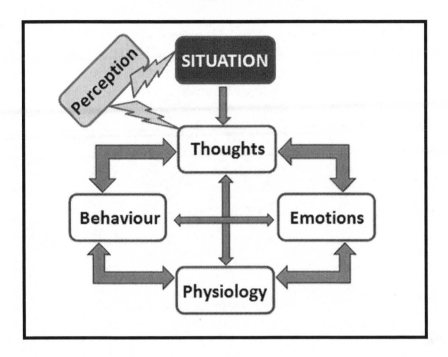

Figure 2

You often can't stop a situation happening, but you do have full control over what it means to you and subsequently how you feel and what you do about it. Whether you see a situation as positive or negative, whether you take the learning and move forward or let it engulf you, it's a choice, your choice, no one else's.

Here is a little experiment in perception; you may have seen this before as it's commonly used in order to demonstrate differences in perception.

What do you see when you look at this picture? (Figure 3)

Figure 3

Some people see two people facing each other; other people see a chalice or large cup. There's no right or wrong answer; it's simply down to perception. Ask someone else what he or she sees - do they see the same thing as you?

I always get good examples to illustrate the differences in perception when I run Outplacement workshops for my corporate clients. These are Career Management programmes designed for people whose jobs are either at risk of redundancy or have been made redundant. I start the programme by ascertaining how each person feels and it never ceases to amaze me how the situation i.e. losing or potentially losing their job, is the same for everyone but how differently each person views it. There are three typical responses:

- *Delegate 1* - "Bring it on! I can finally get to do what I've always wanted to do." *(Excitement/happiness - positive)*

- *Delegate 2* - "Oh my goodness, it's the end of the world, I'll never get another job and then I'll run out of money and then I'll lose my house!" *(Despair/fear - negative)*

- *Delegate 3* - "I'm not really bothered, something will come up." *(Indifference – neutral)*

The fact remains that the situation is the same for all of them; their role has or is likely to end. It isn't right or wrong, good or bad, it is what it is - it's the meaning that they put to it that affects their emotions and their subsequent actions.

It's the same principle when someone does something nice for us; we often feel a nice warm feeling of happiness and even a sense of belonging or we may think, "What do they want?" When someone forgets to do something or doesn't do it to our exacting standards, we can feel aggrieved and hard done to when there may be a perfectly good reason for it. It actually has nothing to do with what the person has or hasn't done, but has everything to do with the meaning we put to it.

We can sometimes perceive others' behaviour as mean and hurtful, when it's only our perception. I had one client who was concerned that his boss was angry with him and he was so worried that he convinced himself that he couldn't go into work the next day because he was going to be fired. When I asked him what had happened to make him think that, he said that his manager was short with him that morning and didn't thank him when he gave him a report that he'd asked for.

I asked how he knew that his manager was angry with him and what evidence he had to support that thought. He had to admit that he didn't have any tangible evidence, which actually helped to calm him down. In his next session, I asked him how his relationship was with his manager and he said, "Oh, I'd forgotten about that, it wasn't anything to do with me, it turned out that he'd had a row with his wife before he left for work and snapped at me". My client's manager wasn't angry with him, which was his *perception* and not based on facts.

If you're easily upset by what people say or do, it's often because you've interpreted their meaning based on your filters rather than on reality. Remember when your parents used to tell you to tell bullies, "Sticks and stones may break my bones but words can never harm me"? They were right. It's only when you put meaning to words and actions that they produce a positive or negative emotion in you.

EXERCISE 12

CHOOSE THE MEANING

The next time something happens that's uncomfortable or upsetting take a step back and actively *choose* how you see it. If you consciously change your perception of a situation, you'll find that your feelings and emotions will change as a result.

Ask yourself:

- What else could this mean?

- How do I know this situation/thought to be true?

- What positives are there in this situation?

- What can I do to turn it into a positive?

- What else could this mean?

- What can I learn from it?

- What can I do differently?

Whilst you may not have been able to stop the situation from occurring, you can certainly choose how you think and feel about it and the actions you take as a result.

YOUR INNER CRITIC

How do you talk to yourself? Is it positive or negative? Have you ever actually listened to your internal dialogue? Some people don't even realise that they do talk to themselves. Occasionally when I ask a client this question they will say, "What are you talking about, I'm not crazy, I don't talk to myself!" Their internal voice is such a part of them that they don't question it or even realise that they have it, let alone have control over it.

Your inner critic is the voice inside you that tells you...

- "You're not good enough."

- "People like me don't do things like that".

- "It's alright for other people they have the skills/backing/money/support that I don't."

- "It's going to be too hard."

- "You're so stupid."

- "You're such an idiot."

- "You're so fat."

- "I'll never do it, so why start?"

This type of negative self-talk puts us into learnt helplessness and prevents us from taking action, as we literally talk ourselves out of doing something based on what our inner critic is saying.

Stop for a minute and actually listen to what your internal voice is saying right now. More importantly, *how* is it talking to you? Is it kind and loving, or nasty and cruel, is it sympathetic or angry, is it positive or negative? Would you let someone else talk to you the way you're letting your inner voice talk to you?

When I do this exercise with clients, so many of them are shocked at how nasty and negative their internal voice is. We have a choice in how we speak to ourselves, yet so often we stumble blindly through our day wondering why we feel stressed and upset at the end of it, totally oblivious to the fact that we've been consistently nasty to ourselves from the moment we woke up ... no wonder we have bad days!

The easiest way to combat that critical inner voice is to take some immediate action. This usually stops that critical voice because, as I've explained before, *the mind can't think of two things at once*, so whilst you focus on action, you can't think of the reasons not to do something.

SILENCE YOUR INNER CRITIC

When you have a particularly critical inner voice, noticing where the voice comes from can give you a good idea about where that thought originated. If the voice comes from behind, I find it's usually the voice of an adult and can be very critical. When I ask clients to listen carefully to that voice, the tone and exactly what it's saying, they often tell me that they can almost hear the voice of their father or mother or some other adult figure that had a strong influence on their upbringing.

If the voice comes from in front, it's usually your inner child talking and the voice tends to be quite different. It's often more whiney and crying, and is usually objecting to having to do something. Clients tell me that they have internal arguments with themselves, their 'adult' voice arguing with the 'child' voice. Internal arguments can to go something like this:

Parent   "You should really be doing something about that."

Child   "But I don't want to, I'm tired."

Parent   "But it's up to you to sort this, you're such a failure."

Child   "I shouldn't have to, why do *I* have to always deal with these things."

If you have an unhelpful internal critic and you would like to stop that ongoing negative chatter, try the following exercise - it may seem a little strange at first, but it really does work.

EXERCISE 13

SILENCE YOUR INNER CRITIC

When you notice your inner voice speaking negatively in a whiney or critical voice:

1. Put your arm out in front of you (it doesn't matter which one), hold up your thumb.

2. Take that inner voice from wherever it is currently and project it to the end of your thumb and wiggle it around.

3. Change the sound of the voice; make it sound like Donald Duck or Mickey Mouse (my particularly favourite is a complaining teenager, that horrible whiney voice they do when they don't want to do something - it works wonders for me).

If you're in public, it may be a little difficult to do the thumb bit, if that's the case, just change the voice to anything that you find comical and don't do the thumb bit – it will have the same effect.

As soon as you do this, you'll notice that the voice completely loses any power it had instantly and the words mean nothing. In fact, it may make you think you're a bit silly for feeling threatened or upset by your own voice.

Before I learnt about my critical inner voice and started to use this technique, I was horrible to myself, I would say some of the most dreadful things consistently throughout the day. As soon as I discovered this technique, it changed everything - it was actually one of my major 'ah-ha' moments. From the second I found out about it, I started to notice and correct anything I was saying to myself that was negative.

I still slip from time to time, which is when I simply change the critical voice to that of a whiney teenager (I don't need to do the thumb) and it works immediately. It just makes me laugh - you can't take anything seriously when it's said in funny voice. It just reminds me that it's *me* saying those words, not some mystical being *and* that those words aren't true ... *I* made them up!

KEY LEARNING POINTS

1. THOUGHTS BECOME THINGS

- We have between 50,000 and 70,000 thoughts a day, up to 95% of thoughts are the same ones as we had the day before - therefore, noticing them and changing them quickly is important to our wellbeing.

- **YOU** create your thoughts.

- Because you create your thoughts, it means that you can also control and change them.

2. YOU CAN'T HAVE TWO THOUGHTS AT ONCE

- Two thoughts can't co-exist.

- Replace negative thoughts with positive ones as soon as you notice them.

- If you stop a negative thought as soon as you notice it, you'll stop the negative spiralling effect that negative thoughts tend to create.

- *Like attracts like* - As negative thoughts attract more of the same, likewise more positive thoughts attract more positive ones.

3. HOW TO CHANGE YOUR THOUGHTS

- You can change your negative thoughts using specific techniques. A soon as you notice the thought:

  o Visualise something positive - the more you practise visualising something that makes you happy, the easier it will be to access that picture quickly, changing negative thoughts to positive, instantly.

  o Use an elastic band and snap it on your wrist.

  o Shout "STOP", stamp your foot or clap your hands together.

  o Get up and move around - do something different – *motion creates emotion* so changing what you're doing will change your thoughts and emotions.

- These techniques are pattern interrupts i.e. they interrupt the pattern of your negative thinking. The more you do them, the harder it will be to access the negative thoughts as you'll be creating new neural pathways.

4. RECURRING THOUGHTS

- If you're having negative thoughts, look to see if there is a message - if there is, deal with it and the thought will be likely to stop.

- If there is no message 'wave' the thought on.

5. UNHELPFUL THINKING PATTERNS

- Unhelpful thinking patterns are patterns of thinking that you've practised so many times that they come automatically.

- They are often called cognitive distortions as they are thoughts that are distorted by your poor patterns of thinking and past programming.

- Identifying your unhelpful thought patterns will help you realise when your thinking is distorted – visit **www.thoughtsbecomethings.co.uk** for access to worksheets you can use to help identify your unhelpful thinking patterns.

6. THE POWER OF PERCEPTION

- Every situation is neutral until we put meaning to it making it good or bad, positive or negative.

- Try looking at situations differently, instead of immediately jumping to conclusions; ask yourself what else it could mean.

- Get into the habit of questioning your perceptions of situations and asking good questions.

7. YOUR INNER CRITIC

- We all have internal dialogue whether we realise it or not

- Listen to how you talk to yourself - is it positive or negative, nurturing or upsetting?

- You create your internal self talk – if your internal talk is negative, it's *you* saying nasty things to yourself no-one else.

- Ask yourself whether you would you let others talk to you the way you talk to yourself?

- If you aren't talking to yourself in a positive way, change the pitch, tone and speed, make the voice sound comical - changing the sound will decrease the intensity of the words.

CHAPTER 5

"The mind can't tell the difference between what's real and what's vividly imagined"

HOW TO CHANGE YOUR EMOTIONS QUICKLY

Do you ever wish that you didn't feel so tired, or that you could change how you're feeling or simply feel more positive?

As we've already discussed there is a close link between what you do with your body and your emotions. In fact, your physiology (body language, facial expressions, breathing etc) and your emotions are so inextricably linked that if you want to immediately change your 'state' (how you're feeling) you can do it rapidly simply through changing your physiology.

Some of our physiology, such as walking, talking and how we hold our body is within our control and is driven by our conscious mind and therefore, we can change it if we want to. Other behaviours are controlled entirely by our subconscious e.g. going red when we feel embarrassed. In terms of our brain, our limbic system is where our base emotions and most of our automatic body language originates - it's the limbic system that's responsible for our fight or flight response. The fight or flight response is a physiological reaction that occurs in response to a perceived harmful event, attack, or threat to survival.

Often men and women who suffer extreme stress over prolonged periods (i.e. they are consistently triggering their flight/fight response) may experience reproductive issues, as their body constantly diverts resources away from that area to other larger organs that need it. This process occurs in the limbic system and happens completely unconsciously. People who receive a shock suddenly go pale - again this is because the subconscious is diverting blood away from the skin, to other important organs in preparation for flight or flight. This proves interconnectedness between thoughts and physiology.

CHANGE YOUR STATE

If I said, "Behind door A is someone who is depressed, describe how they look", you would probably say, "Head low, shoulders slumped, shallow breathing, sad expression..." and if I said,

"Behind door B is someone who's really happy, describe how they look", you would say the opposite, head up, eyes bright, happy expression etc. Whatever emotions you experience, your body follows and vice versa. The great thing about having this information is that in any moment you can change how you feel by changing your physiology.

Shortly after I first came across this concept, I was driving home after a 12-hour day thinking how tired I was and then I remembered about changing my physiology to change my state. I looked at my body language and noticed I was slumped, my shoulders were down and I was bent over, my blinking had slowed and I was yawning every couple of minutes (yawning is our body's way of taking in more oxygen as our breath is more shallow when we're tired). I immediately adjusted my body, sat up straight, opened my eyes fully and took a few big deep breaths, smiled and instantly felt differently. I was actually quite shocked at the difference simply adjusting my body language and *deciding* not to be tired could make to improve my mood.

I use this technique constantly now, with both my clients and myself. It's especially useful to use with workshop delegates in the dreaded afternoon 'slump slot' just after lunch. I get them to do an exercise that involves moving their body - *motion creates emotion* - and they are then usually much more awake and receptive to learning more.

Since I learnt this technique, whenever I find myself slipping into any old negative physiology patterns, I sit up straight, put my shoulders back, smile and take a deep breath. It's so simple, but makes a massive difference.

EXERCISE 14

CHANGE YOUR EMOTIONS BY CHANGING YOUR PHYSIOLOGY

For the next 3 days, keep an eye on how you're feeling. If you start to feel any negativity, observe what you're doing with your physiology (your body, face, how you're breathing etc) and change it. Put your shoulders back, sit/stand up straight, take a deep breath in and smile.

You'll be amazed at how quickly you move from negativity to positivity and the more you practise this, the better at it you'll become. It interrupts your usual negative pattern and again, will create new neural pathways moving you towards a naturally positive state.

MOTION CREATES EMOTION

Changing your physiology by getting up and moving is a great way to change your emotions especially if you're stressed or anxious. Putting some distance between you and the problem can be beneficial when experiencing strong negative emotions such as anger or frustration. When anger starts to rise, your body sends out a shot of adrenalin, that goes back to the 'flight or fight' response, which is what prepares us to either run away from a threat or fight it. These days, however, we can't run away from issues or fight, so we end up with large amounts of adrenalin coursing through our veins with nowhere for it to go. Those unused chemicals contribute towards aggression, anxiety, stress and if not addressed over the long term, can lead to depression as well as physical illnesses.

Getting your body moving will create changes in your biochemistry, which will counterbalance the effects of the adrenalin, and other chemicals released into the bloodstream when we experience strong negative emotions.

MANAGING ANGER & OTHER NEGATIVE EMOTIONS

Start to tune into your body, often there will be early warning signs like quickening of your heartbeat or tightness in your chest or sweating palms that alert you to the fact that you're about to experience negative emotions.

Learn to notice these signs and excuse yourself immediately even if that means that you look a bit odd doing so (it's better to do that than potentially experiencing other harmful consequences) and go to the washroom or take a walk, preferably outside where you can get some fresh air. Removing yourself from the situation and the simple act of moving your body will help defuse those negative emotions. It also acts as a pattern interrupt, as we've discussed previously, if you keep interrupting your old patterns of behaviour, you'll develop new ones and it will become more difficult to access the old ones.

If you can't actually physically remove yourself from a situation, try *visualising* going for a walk. To illustrate this, a client was explaining to me that she couldn't just get up and take a walk when she was feeling stressed or frustrated in an important meeting. However, she recognised the need to take a step back and disassociate herself from what was going on, at least for a short time. Therefore, she developed a method of *visualising* going for a walk that really works for her.

She explained that she literally 'shuts down' in her mind for as long as it takes for her to mentally get up out of her seat, walk to the door, open it, walk to the stairs, walk down the stairs, out of reception, walk around the block once (twice if she is feeling particularly stressed) come back into the building, back up the stairs and back in the room and ready to re-join the discussion.

She says that no one knows what she is doing; they assume that she has zoned out for a while and is taking 'thinking' time. When she has done this little 'visualisation walk', she says that she has usually calmed down and is ready to join the discussion again with a more balanced viewpoint.

TAKE A HIKE & CHANGE YOUR BIOCHEMISTY

Regular exercise is an amazing way to help you gain a more balanced perspective on any situation and to help you manage your emotions, as it helps burn off those unwanted chemicals produced by the flight or fight response. That's why exercise is often prescribed for sufferers of depression; it literally changes your biochemistry.

Cortisol is a hormone produced by the body under stress, such as anger, anxiety or fear and over a prolonged period it ultimately inflames and damages your organs. Exercise burns cortisol and adrenalin and leaving us healthier and happier. Exercise also stimulates the brain's pituitary gland to release endorphins into the bloodstream, calming us down and making us feel good. Endorphins are morphine-like hormone molecules that enter the brain's neurons and park on receptors that normally send pain–killing molecules back to other parts of the brain. It is thought that endorphins are even more powerful and yield a more euphoric feeling than opiate drugs such as morphine and opium, which park on the same receptors when introduced to the body.

Exercise doesn't have to mean running a marathon or doing an hour's and hour's worth of hard labour in the gym, it can be anything that you do for around 10-20 minutes that increases your heart rate. That's why a walk around the block can be sufficient to make a real difference to the way you're feeling - see Chapter 5 for more on the power of exercise.

ACT LIKE A SUPERHERO!

We've all heard the term *'Fake it 'til you make it'* and actually, there is now evidence that supports that it does actually work. As we've talked about, we can actually trick our brains into producing different emotions by purposely changing our body language to that of the emotion that we want to experience. Even better than that is the fact that not only can we change our mood, but we can actually influence hormone release/biochemistry through changing our physiology.

Recent research has confirmed that adopting a 'power stance' (think of a superhero posture, legs spread, hands on hips, elbows bent, and chin up) conveys a sense of the individual having power. Furthermore, tests have proven that adopting the stance for two minutes affects our release of the hormones testosterone and cortisol.

Why these two hormones?

- *Testosterone* - Research on testosterone in relation to power indicates that testosterone levels increase when we anticipate competing (and it's the same for men and women), as well as after winning, but testosterone levels drop when we lose. In other words, testosterone goes up with the possibility of, or with actual power and decreases when power, or the opportunity to attain power, is lost.

- *Cortiso*l - Sometimes referred to as a 'stress hormone' because its levels often rise with stress. People who are powerful or hold powerful positions tend to have lower baseline levels of cortisol and, when stressed, their cortisol levels don't rise as much as in people who are relatively powerless or perceive that they are.

EXERCISE 15

INCREASE YOUR POWER

Whenever you want to increase your power (confidence, self esteem etc) you simply need to do this exercise in order to trick your mind and body into actually experiencing physiological changes and supercharging your performance:

1. Stand up tall and strong with your feet part.

2. Put your hands on your hips.

3. Tighten your stomach muscles.

4. Put your shoulders back and push your chest out.

5. Lift your chin.

6. Take a deep breath and say, "I'm magnificent!"

7. If you can, actually walk around taking big confident strides (you could even imagine a Superhero cape on your back if you like!).

8. Hold this stance for two minutes and you'll have no option but to feel more powerful - as your physiology will automatically change your biochemistry.

I appreciate that you may feel a little silly doing this, but it really does work and all the research is there if you want to read it for yourself, just Google "Superman Stance". I teach this to clients who would like to be more confident in difficult conditions such as giving presentations or in an interview situation. I urge my more nervous clients to go to the washroom before they are about to give their presentation/interview (if there isn't anywhere else that they can be alone) and stand in a cubical for two minutes doing the 'Superhero Stance'. OK, it may not be the best venue, but the results will be the same; you'll feel more confident and think thoughts that are more positive.

Stand like a superhero, feel like a superhero, act like superhero!

WHY WE SOMETIMES GO 'BLANK'

Are you one of those people who sometimes can't think quickly enough when someone says something that shocks or upsets you and afterwards you think, "Why didn't I say X, Y, Z"? It's a common response and something that I experience from time to time, so I can appreciate how frustrating it is.

What's happening is that when the subconscious receives distressing information it literally freezes for a moment while it processes it. A second or so later, your conscious brain will kick in and you'll be able to respond but it's often too late and you've missed an opportunity to say what you really think.

If you know this happens to you, the next time you 'freeze', instead of trying to answer a question or give a coherent reply, tell the person that you need to think about what they have said and will get back to them. I tend to say, "I hear what you've said, I just need to process it. Can I come back to you?" That buys me some time to think of an appropriate response. It's a common problem and often knowing that there is a reasonable explanation for it helps us understand it and deal with it in a more effective way.

THE POWER OF WORDS

The words we use are incredibly powerful and directly affect our thoughts, which in turn affect our emotions and ultimately our behaviour and so the spiral begins. The people around us generally influence our language, not just as we grow up, but all the way through our lives. For example, you may have grown up in a household where swearing was acceptable, however, in your workplace, it may not be. You therefore, find alternative words to express your emotions and with enough use, the new language will become your norm.

Using strong words will actually produce strong emotions and once we start to use specific language to describe our emotions, it becomes habitual. A good example of this was recently when a friend of mine told me about a problem with her daughter. I said, "Sounds like a bit of a nightmare" She replied, "It's just a hiccup, it's nowhere near a nightmare!"

I thought the difference in our language was interesting, to me her problem was a 'nightmare', whereas to her it was a mere 'hiccup'. That got me thinking about the power of the language we use. Was 'nightmare' a throw-back from my childhood when *everything* was a problem for my parents? Had I picked up dramatic language that's not applicable or appropriate and is it making my life worse than it needs to be because *we experience the emotions that our language creates*?

If, instead of using a strong emotional word such as 'angry', e.g. "I'm really *angry* about that", what would happen if you changed that word to something less emotional such as 'irritated', e.g. "I'm a bit *irritated* about that". Would you feel the same and would it create the same emotion and behaviour in you? I don't think so. We can only experience a feeling if we actually use the word that describes it – i.e. we can't feel depressed if we don't 'label' the feeling as depressed, or we can't feel angry if we don't use the word 'angry'.

If you know that you use dramatic language, I'd like you to try the following exercise:

EXERCISE 16

CHANGE YOUR WORDS

Make a list of the top ten negative or dramatic words that you use on a consistent basis. Next to each one write a word that you could use to replace it - a word that has less intensity of feeling to it. (I've given you a couple of examples to start you off):

OLD WORD	NEW WORD
Devastated	Upset
Angry	Disappointed
Nightmare	Hiccup
1.	
2.	
3.	
4.	
5.	
6.	

7.		
8.		
9.		
10.		

Once you have your list (don't worry if you don't get to ten, you can always keep adding to the list as you find yourself using strong words) keep it with you, regularly review it and use your new words wherever you can to replace the old. The more you use the new words to describe your emotions, the deeper the neural pathway will become and eventually, you won't need to think about it at all, the new words will become second nature.

Also, notice how different you feel using the new words. Check in with yourself to see if it's making a difference, you should feel calmer and more in control. If you don't, then maybe you need to review your new words and change them for something with even less intensity.

Visit www.thoughtsbecomethings.co.uk and sign up to receive a template that you can use to note and keep track of your unhelpful words.

SPEAK ONLY IN POSITIVE TERMS

Our brains literally do not recognise the word 'don't' and therefore, it's important to state your intentions in the positive e.g. if you tell a child, "Mind you don't trip", their brain won't register the 'don't' and they are likely to trip. Similarly, if you tell yourself, 'don't' do something your brain simply won't accept the 'don't' and will deliver whatever it is you've asked for. For example, if you say to yourself, "Don't fall" you're almost guaranteed to fall.

What you need to consciously do is state things in the positive and remove the word 'don't' from your vocabulary as much as possible, e.g. instead of telling your child, "Be careful you don't trip" say, "Walk carefully" or instead of, "Don't drop that" say, "Carry that with both hands" - we get what we think about so stating our intent in positive terms is important.

Start to pay close noticing the language of the people around you. Do they use negative or strong, inappropriate language (and I'm not just talking about swearing here) to describe how they are feeling? The more time we spend with others, the more we are likely to adopt their language patterns subconsciously, so make sure that you *consciously* choose your language and only adopt other peoples' language if it's positive.

ARE YOU 'SHOULDING' ALL OVER YOURSELF?

Another set of words that affect our thoughts and behaviours are 'should', 'must' and 'ought'. We've already covered these words in 'Unhelpful Thought Patterns' section in Chapter 4; however, as we're talking about words here, I think it's worth mentioning again. These three words literally shut you down from achieving. When you say you *should, must* or *ought* to be doing something, what you really mean and what you're actually telling yourself is that you have no intention of doing it. 'Should', 'must' and 'ought' is the language of a procrastinator.

When we use those words in relation to other people, we tend to be judging them, putting our rules onto them and we have unrealistic expectations about them e.g. "They *shouldn't* be doing that, they *ought* be doing this", which will ultimately leave you feeling disappointed leading to a certain level of pain.

If you consciously take the words *'should', 'must'* and *'ought'* out of your vocabulary, you're much more likely to actually get off your backside and do the things you've been putting off and stop making yourself feel bad or guilty for procrastinating. There is a well-known saying in the NLP world that sums it up nicely:

"Stop Shoulding All over Yourself"

THE POWER OF VISUALISATION

I can't stress enough the power that visualisation has on our lives as *the mind can't tell the difference between something that's vividly imagined and something that's real.* Therefore, the more you practise visualising the outcome you want, the more likely you are to achieve it. The great thing about it is that it's easy to do, you can do it anywhere and no-one needs to know you're doing it.

Visualising something actually creates new neural pathways in the brain as we discussed in Chapter 3. When you do something for the first time whether you do it for real or you visualise doing it, you create a new neural pathway. The more times you practise doing that thing, visualising it clearly in your mind then the deeper the neural pathway will become and the easier it will be to do in real life.

There has been so much research done into the power of visualisation, you only need to look online and you'll find pages and pages of evidence. Neuroscientists at Harvard carried out a piece of research where they taught a simple five-fingered combination of piano notes to a group of people, which they physically played over and over again for two hours a day for five consecutive days. Another group of volunteers didn't actually play the notes, but imagined playing the same combination for the same practise time each day.

The researchers examined the brains of the volunteers every day using a technique known as TMS (Transcranial Magnetic Stimulation) and found that there was little or no difference between the brains of those who actually played the notes and those who visualised playing them. The brain areas in both cases grew significantly in size.

VISUALISATION IN SPORT

Visualisation is a huge part of coaching in any sport; it has been proven to increase performance levels considerably. I've worked with semi-professional golfers who have significantly decreased their handicap through the visualisation techniques that I've taught them.

I start by asking them to talk me through a typical shot. By understanding what they are thinking and saying to themselves before, during and after the shot, I can recognise where their game can be improved. Often they will tell me that they are saying things like, "Don't miss, don't miss!" the problem with that is that as I mentioned previously, our brain will literally disregard the 'don't' and will give us exactly what we've asked for, i.e. to miss!

Another client told me that he continually visualised hitting the ball into the bunker and would repeat to himself, "Don't hit the bunker. Don't hit the bunker!" The problem with that was that he was literally commanding himself through his words and pictures to hit the bunker which he did very successfully and on a consistent basis.

I then ask clients to visualise and talk me through a perfect shot creating a mini video in their minds. I encourage them to see, feel and hear everything they do before, during and after the perfect shot in as much detail as possible, right down to how the breeze feels on their skin and what sounds they can hear around them, exactly what they see and how they are feeling. I get them totally 'in the zone' so that they are fully associated with their thoughts and feelings. This creates strong neural pathways, even though they are only *visualising* the perfect shot.

I do this exercise with them a number of times so that they can easily access the video in their mind whenever they think of it. I then tell them to go away and run their video; mentally practising getting the perfect shot as many times as they possibly can before their next game. I'm happy to say that every person I've taught this exercise to has lowered his or her handicap without fail. *We get what we think about!*

This technique works in every sport, you simply have to

visualise your perfect outcome in as much detail as possible including what you see, what you hear and how you feel - totally absorbing yourself into your 'video' and play it over and over again. I guarantee that if you do this exercise repeatedly alongside your physical practising, you'll see positive results.

VISUALISE THE OUTCOME YOU DESIRE

You can use the same visualisation technique for any important event where you may be nervous or if you have to produce an outstanding performance. If a client has an important meeting, presentation or interview etc, I always tell them to visualise the whole day from beginning to end and to *visualise it going perfectly*. Visualise your whole day in as much detail as possible from getting up, to getting dressed, to getting to the venue and setting up, giving your presentation/interview etc and everything else that you're planning to do that day.

Don't forget that it's important to visualise *everything going perfectly* - if you visualise anything negative, then that's what you're likely to experience when you come to the real thing. The more you visualise things going perfectly, by the time you come to the real thing, your mind already knows what to expect and exactly what you need to do because you've programmed it into your subconscious i.e. you've built a deep neural pathway.

If you feel nervous, which is natural, do the deep breathing exercise explained later in this chapter. Calm yourself down and let your subconscious take over - it's almost like switching to autopilot if you've practised visualising everything going well enough beforehand.

VISUALISATION & WORRY

If you're a worrier, I'm guessing that you picture all the worst-case scenarios in microscopic detail. What you're actually doing when you're visualising all the catastrophes that *may* happen to you, is training your brain to react in a negative way and you're creating deep neural pathways that make it easy to go into that 'victim' state which actually attracts negative outcomes.

A client of mine had to give a speech at her daughter's wedding and she was terrified - in fact, she was so upset that she actually cried while she was telling me about it and found it difficult to get her words out. When I asked her what she was seeing (visualising) and what she was saying to herself when she thought about giving the speech, she said, "I've been trying to think about all the things that could go wrong so that if they do go wrong on the day, I'll be prepared". I was horrified, what she was actually doing was programming herself for it to go wrong and having all the negative feelings and behaviours that went with it!

Because (again) *the mind can't tell the difference between what's real and what's vividly imagined* she was fully associated with it all going horribly wrong, she was upsetting herself to the point that she could barely speak. I told her she had to reverse her thinking and visualise everything going perfectly.

I got her to relax and visualise how the day would go if everything were perfect, I asked to see, feel and hear everything going well in as much detail as possible creating a mini video in her mind. We did this a number of times until she could access the 'video' clearly, instantly. I then told her to practise running that video as many times as she could prior to the wedding and to practise some simple confidence techniques that I had also taught her.

She texted me on the evening of the wedding and told me that she had been completely in control of her emotions (although she did have a little cry in the church, but that was an appropriate response, and so she was happy) and the speech went perfectly. Since then I'm happy to say that as a result of that short one hour session with me, not only did her speech go well, but she is now able to stand up and present in front of people comfortably, something she has never been able to do before. Consequently, she has been able to expand her business by delivering profitable training sessions to other businesses, something that she would never have been able to do previously because of her irrational fear of public speaking.

Not only does visualising something going well repeatedly significantly increase your chances of success, doing something over and over in your mind will also help you to spot and overcome any obstacles, allowing you the chance to change things before they become a problem. It really is the difference between success and failure – it unlocks hidden potential.

The following exercise is a really simple way to demonstrate the power of visualisation:

EXERCISE 17

THE POWER OF VISUALISATION

Read this exercise through at least once before trying it so that you understand what you need to do:

1. Stand up straight with your feet, hips, torso and head all facing the front.

2. Take your right arm and point forward at right angles to your body.

3. Twist your body around so that you're pointing as far as you

can possibly reach behind you.

4. Make a mental note how far you've managed to point.

5. Return back and put your arm down.

6. Close your eyes (sit down while you do this if you find you're a little unsteady standing up with your eyes closed) and imagine pointing much further - visualise clearly in your mind the new position that you want to point to.

7. Open your eyes and repeat numbers 1-5 and note where you are now able to point to.

Did you point much further after the visualisation? I'm sure you did. If this simple exercise demonstrates how much further you can point as a result of visualising the outcome you want (albeit simply pointing), imagine how much more you can achieve in your life if you adopt the habit of visualising achieving what you want on a consistent basis.

If you ask any successful person, they will tell you they imagined creating their multi-million selling widget or they have visualised running a multi-national corporation or "always dreamed" of owning their own business. Everything starts with a thought and visualising how you want your life to be whether you're consciously aware of it or not. *THOUGHTS BECOME THINGS!*

RELAXATION TECHNIQUES

Learning simple relaxation techniques is important to controlling your emotions and to dealing with and releasing stress, anxiety and tension. I've listed a few techniques that are simple to do and give immediate results. Obviously, the more you practise them, the easier they become and the quicker you'll find yourself in control of your emotions and in a relaxed state.

PROGRESSIVE MUSCLE RELAXATION

Progressive muscle relaxation is a technique that helps to release tension in the muscles bringing about deep feelings of relaxation. It's best done either sitting or lying down in a quiet place, preferably where you won't be disturbed. Wearing loose, comfortable clothing would also be beneficial. It's a great technique to do if you have trouble getting off to sleep. Therefore, getting into the habit of doing it in bed, as part of your bedtime routine, is perfect.

EXERCISE 18

FULL MUSCLE RELAXATION METHOD

Please read this whole exercise at least twice before you try it. The technique involves grouping the body into muscle groups i.e. legs, mid section, arms and head and systematically tensing and releasing each muscle in its muscle group, only moving on to the next muscle group once the current one feels totally relaxed. If you do this exercise fully, it should take around 20 minutes (if you haven't already fallen asleep part way through!).

You will tense each muscle twice, once for 5 seconds and then relax for 15 seconds and then tense that muscle again for a further 5 seconds, release again for 15 seconds and then move on to the next muscle. As you tense your muscles, pay close attention to any sensations that you may be experiencing in the muscles as they contract.

1. Starting with the feet and legs: tense and relax first your toes, then feet, then calf muscles, inner thighs, thighs and buttocks using the pattern mentioned above - then tense and relax the muscle group as a whole.

2. Moving to your arms: tense and relax your fingers, then your

173

hands biceps, triceps and your full arm - then tense and relax the muscle group as a whole.

3. Moving to your mid section: tense and relax your pelvic floor muscles, then your stomach and then your chest - then tense and relax the muscle group as a whole

4. Moving to your back: tense your lower back and then your upper back - then tense and relax the muscle group as a whole.

5. Moving to your head: tense and release your neck, then your facial muscles, the top of your head - then tense and relax the muscle group as a whole.

Once all the muscles in each section have been tensed and released twice you should experience a feeling of deep relaxation.

The following exercise is a modified version of the above relaxation method which can be used if you don't have 20 minutes or if you've thoroughly practised the full version and are looking for a quicker way to relax:

EXERCISE 19

MODIFIED MUSCLE RELAXATION METHOD

This shortened version involves tensing and releasing whole muscle groups rather than breaking down the individual muscles in each group. It should take around 5 minutes to complete.

Please read this whole exercise twice before you try the technique.

Tense each full muscle group twice once for 5 seconds and then relax for 15 seconds and then tense that muscle group again for another 5 seconds, releasing for 15 seconds, before moving on to the next muscle group. As you tense your muscles pay close attention to any sensations that you may be experiencing in the muscles as they contract.

1. Starting with the feet and legs: tense and relax all your muscles from your toes to your buttocks using the pattern described above.

2. Moving to your arms: tense and relax all your muscles from your fingers to your biceps, triceps and shoulders.

3. Moving to your mid section: tense and relax all the muscles

from your pelvic floor to your chest.

4. Moving to your back: tense and release all the muscles including your lower and upper back.

5. Moving to your head: tense and release all the muscles in this group from your neck and face to the top of your head.

Once all the muscles in each section have been tensed and released twice you should experience a feeling of deep relaxation. Using this modified technique may be more practical and help you to calm down quickly in real-life situations, where lying down with your eyes closed for 20 minutes isn't an option.

DEEP BREATHING

When we experience intense emotions like anxiety, anger or panic our breathing tends to be very shallow and quick which can make us feel dizzy and confused. I especially recommend deep breathing for clients who are about to undergo potentially stressful situations such as interviews, presentations or before an important meeting or difficult conversation. It can equally be used when the kids are driving you crazy or you're feeling overly anxious or overwhelmed. Doing this exercise can help bring some perspective back to a situation and help to calm you down. The beauty of it is that you can do it anywhere, at any time and no one knows you're doing it.

EXERCISE 20

DEEP BREATHING

Take 10 deep breaths – in and out counts as one breath. These breaths must come from the stomach (diaphragm) and not from the chest i.e. your stomach should extend fully on the 'in' breath and contract fully on the out breath – think of a baby, they breathe from their stomach, it's only as we get older that we tend to breathe from our chests.

By the time you get to the sixth or seventh breath, physiological changes happen within the body as stress release hormones are pumped into your body which calms you down. The old adage of 'take 10 breaths' to calm down before you do something or say something when you're angry or frustrated is actually based on fact, it works.

CHANGE UNHELPFUL SLEEP PATTERNS

When we experience consistent negative emotions such as stress, anxiety and depression, we often find that our sleep patterns are interrupted. This is a common complaint with many people, especially those who are going through significant life changes e.g. redundancy, job change, marriage/relationship break-up, moving house etc. The majority of my clients tell me that they don't have a problem actually falling asleep but they tend to wake up about 2.00 or 3.00 am and find it difficult to go back to sleep, only managing to get back to sleep about half an hour before their alarm goes off.

Before I give you some tools to combat your poor sleeping, it's important to understand what happens when we sleep. The following chart explains our sleep cycle:

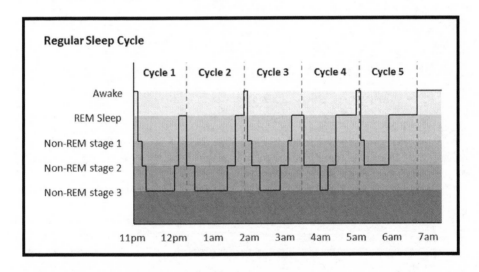

During non-REM sleep, the body repairs and re-grows tissues, builds bone and muscle, and strengthens the immune system. During REM sleep all of our memories are consolidated, particularly our procedural and spatial memory. We tend to spend more time than usual in REM sleep following days when we've been in unusual situations requiring us to learn many new tasks. Although most people don't tend to wake after each cycle of REM, if we're over-stimulated, we may wake up fully and it may take the length of an entire sleep cycle to get back to sleep. It's assumed that REM sleep and the dreams we have during REM sleep is physiologically necessary for our healthy brain function.

During REM sleep, the subconscious sorts out all the experiences we've had during the previous day. To use a common metaphor, it literally files everything away neatly in boxes. Problems occur when your subconscious can't find the right 'box' in which to file an item; that item will usually be something that you haven't been able to resolve during the day.

If you tend to wake at the end of the second sleep cycle (as most of my clients with non-diagnosed sleep problems tend to do) one of the easiest ways to get back to sleep quickly, is to leave a notepad by the side of the bed and if you awaken, worrying about something, write it down as quickly as possible. Once you've done that, it's usually enough to assure the subconscious that the item it couldn't 'file' has been resolved, allowing you to go straight back to sleep.

Don't leave it too long to write anything down after you wake, or stimulate yourself too much by getting out of bed or turning on the TV, because if you do, you may find that you have to wait until the next sleep cycle is due before you fall asleep again (typically 1.5-2 hours).

Whenever I teach this simple technique to clients, most tell me that they only needed to do it for a couple of nights and then they stop waking up in the middle of the night and have a much more restful sleep.

HOW TO GET A GOOD NIGHT'S SLEEP

Here are some other tips for a restful night's sleep - try No 1 first and then move on to No 2 etc:

1. *Change your bed time:*

   - For 2 weeks, put your bed time back by an hour (no matter how tired you are) go to bed at the same time every night and get up at the same time every morning - even at weekends.

   - At the end of the 2 weeks, if your sleep pattern is better, go to bed half an hour earlier (don't add the time onto the end of your sleep).

   - At the end of a further 2 weeks, move your bed time forward by a further half an hour.

- Repeat as necessary until you attain the right amount of sleep for you.

2. *Keep a sleep diary:*

- Each morning for a week, keep a note of how many hours you actually spent sleeping. Not how much time you spent in bed, but how much time you actually slept each night.

- For the following 2 weeks, only go to bed for the amount of hours you actually slept each night the previous week i.e. take the time you need to get up and work back the number of hours you've been sleeping. For example, if you've been sleeping for average of 5 hours a night and you usually wake up at 6.00 am, then make your bedtime 1.00 am.

- For the whole of the 2 weeks, go to bed and get up at the same time, even at weekends.

- At the end of the 2 weeks, if your sleep pattern is better, start going to bed half an hour earlier (again, don't add the half an hour on to the end of the sleep, you must add it at the beginning).

- Every 2 weeks, go to bed half an hour earlier until you find the right amount of sleep for you.

- Visit www.thoughtsbecomethings.co.uk and sign up to receive a diary template that you can use to record your sleep patterns.

DO'S AND DON'TS OF A GOOD NIGHT'S SLEEP

DO...

- Set up a good bedtime routine, this could include having a warm bath and/or practising some of the relaxation techniques outlined in this chapter.

- Have a warm drink (not caffeine or alcohol).

- Take regular exercise.

- Go to bed and wake up at the same time every day, even at weekends.

- Make sure the room is not too hot or too cold.

- Make sure that the room is quiet and dark - use ear plugs and a sleep mask if appropriate.

DON'T...

- Drink caffeine or smoke before bed.

- Watch any programmes or films that may get your heart racing directly before bed.

- Have any disagreements with family.

- Play exciting video games directly before bed.

- Exercise just before bed.

- Go to bed too hungry or too full.

- Have the TV on in your bedroom.

- Lie there awake - if you're awake for more than 30 minutes, get up and do something else, only going back to bed when you feel tired enough to sleep - this way you'll be training your mind to know that bed is for sleeping.

- SLEEP DURING THE DAY; NO MATTER HOW TIRED YOU ARE!

These techniques have been tried and tested by my clients and myself over the years and have proven to be very effective. However, if you try these techniques and you still find that you have trouble sleeping, I would always suggest that you seek further advice from your doctor.

THE POWER OF EXERCISE

When we're feeling stressed or anxious or when our work/life balance is out of kilter, one of the first things to go by the wayside can be exercise. However, there is so much evidence to suggest that exercise is not only good for our physical health, but it's also critical for good mental health. As I mentioned earlier, it doesn't mean that you have to flog yourself in the gym. There has been lots of talk in the press lately about the benefits of walking which, according to the NHS website, include a reduction in the risk of chronic illnesses, such as heart disease, Type 2 diabetes, asthma, stroke and some cancers.

As well as physical benefits, there are also many psychological benefits of walking which include:

- *Improved cognitive performance* – Your working memory is better when you're walking than when you're sitting still - working memory is important for reasoning and learning.

- *Improved mood* - Being in daylight improves your mood and general feeling of well-being - positive moods have been linked to more creative thinking.

- *Psychological benefits* - Walking, particularly outside and in nature, can produce psychological benefits within five minutes and have been shown to increase mood and self-esteem.

If you can get out and walk in nature, it helps people who are cognitively exhausted - it helps to restock your mental energy

With all these benefits, there really is no excuse not to get those trainers on and get moving!

EXERCISE AND WORK/LIFE BALANCE

A new client came to me with the goal of achieving a better work life balance. As I do in every first session, I wanted to first understand what had lead to his decision. He told me that he had been continually feeling stressed and under pressure lately - he was forty-four and ran his own successful company that was growing quickly. When I asked him what he did for leisure and how much exercise he was managing to get each week he said, "I work all the time! If I was to exercise, the only time I could do it would be during the day and what kind of an example would I be setting for my staff if they saw me disappearing for a couple of hours to the gym every day?"

He then went on to tell me that he had recently had a heart scare and had he been told by medical staff that if he didn't change his lifestyle, then things could get an awful lot worse. My reply was, "So taking time out of your day - if that's the only time you have - seems pretty critical to me. After all, if you don't look after *you*, there'll be no business!" Luckily, he agreed and we managed to come up with a plan that worked for him. He literally scheduled exercise into his diary as he would any other important meeting and he made those training sessions immovable.

After a couple of months, we reviewed progress and he said that *everything* had changed, not only was he sticking to the plan (because he had made exercise a **must**, not an option) he was feeling much more in control, better able to make decisions, and was feeling much calmer and happier. He also reported that his staff had commented that he was much more pleasant to be around.

Making regular exercise a must and scheduling it into his diary as he would any other important meeting meant that he stuck to the plan and saw many benefits as a result. His employees didn't think badly of him (they were thrilled because he was so much nicer to be around) and as he saw his health improve, his fitness and energy levels increased which made him much more efficient and effective at his job.

SCHEDULE 'ME TIME'

One of the biggest complaints I get, more so from my female clients, is that they're 'losing' themselves and no longer feel important or that they don't have any time for themselves. They tell me that after work, looking after the kids, doing the house work, cooking (well you get the idea) they're exhausted even when they get help from their partners. Another common complaint is that they feel 'unnoticed' and they have 'lost' themselves somewhere along the way. They report feeling burnt out, sometimes they will use words like anxious, stressed, depressed, overwhelmed or out of control.

Invariably when I ask these women what they do just for themselves and for their own wellbeing, they look at me horrified. "For me? I have no time for me!" is a typical response. I'm not being sexist here, it simply isn't an issue that my male clients have raised, they don't tend to have the same emotional issues around feeling unimportant etc as my female clients. However, they will tell me that between their work and home commitments, they don't have enough time to exercise or have any time to relax and reduce their stress levels which can lead to feelings of stress and anxiety.

No matter who you are and what you do, it's important to schedule time specifically for you. By schedule I mean put time in the diary and make it immoveable - to do something just for you. You should use that time to do whatever it is that makes you happy. Exercise is great (as we've discussed), take up a hobby or revisit an old hobby, meet with friends for a glass of wine or coffee, go to the cinema, watch the match, go to a spa, do something that makes you feel good.

When I talk to clients about the possibility of scheduling time for them, at first they can tend to be a bit cautious and will explain that they feel guilty taking time out, on their own without their family. It can feel very uncomfortable for them. Often, they have their own self-imposed reasons for not doing things for themselves. They have created the life that they now have and they decided either consciously or otherwise, not to take time for themselves. Often wrongly imagining that the family can't do without them and that everything will fall apart when they aren't there.

When I explain that NOT taking time out is likely to be damaging them and their family far more than if they did, it tends to provoke a shift in their thinking. If taking some time for yourself will mean that you'll be more in control, less anxious, happier and healthier, how on earth can you *not* schedule 'Me Time'?

If you're feeling happier and healthier, those around you'll also benefit as *behaviour breeds behaviour*. I think it's far more irresponsible to live your life being grumpy, unhappy and unfulfilled, as it will definitely adversely affect your family. As we've discussed many times throughout this book, we learn by modelling others and so, if you have children you're teaching them how to be tired, upset and stressed and that they should practise self-sacrifice. Is that what you want your children to learn? Because there is a good chance that they will grow up displaying exactly the same behaviours as you at some point.

Give some thought to what you want to do with your 'Me Time' and get it scheduled in the diary as an immovable appointment. I must point out here that it's possible that you may encounter some resistance at first. Loved ones may feel a little hurt or surprised that you want to do something that doesn't include them. However, you should stand firm, they will likely change their stance once they see the benefits of a calmer, happier, more in control you. It's the change in routine that they're usually resisting. Typically, people don't like change, simply reassure them and do what you need to do ... for all of you!

STOP THE EXCUSES

"I don't have time" is a common excuse that I often hear from clients for not schedule 'Me Time' or from people who are leading particularly stressful lives. Apart from the fact that you can't afford *not* to make time for yourself, you need to identify whether you're using the time you have in the most effective way. In today's society, we feel that we have to be everything to everyone and we have to be Superman or Superwoman, whereas the smart people are aware of where they spend their time and use it effectively.

THE TIME AUDIT

Completing a Time Audit can be useful in pinpointing where you're spending your time and where you could be using it to better effect.

189

To complete a time audit you need to write down what you do during a day and look for the areas where your time could be better utilised. Here is an example of a part completed Time Audit Form:

TIME	SUNDAY	MONDAY	TUESDAY
6.00 am	Sleep	Got up, showered, dressed	Got up, showered, dressed
7.00 am	Sleep	Got the kids up, made breakfast	Got the kids up, made breakfast
8.00 am	Got up, showered, dressed Made breakfast	Dropped the kids off Went to work	Dropped the kids off Went to work
9.00 am	Cleaned the house Made breakfast	Work	Work

Go to www.thoughtsbecomethings.co.uk and sign up to receive a template Time Audit form that you can complete yourself.

When you do this exercise for a whole week, it will become very clear where the areas are that you could capitalise on. One thing I recommend is to outsource (pay someone else to do it) wherever possible and where you can afford to, things like ironing and cleaning are no-brainers. You can outsource those activities far more cheaply than you would think. Some clients are surprised when I suggest having a cleaner and say that they can't imagine paying for something that they can do themselves. However, when I point out how much their time is worth versus how much it would cost to employ someone to do those more mundane but time consuming tasks, they don't really have much of an argument.

Do a quick calculation of your hourly rate or how much you think your time is worth to you per hour and then research some prices to see how much it would cost to pay someone to do the things you'd rather not do. It's a good way to justify bringing in some outside help, if that's what you need in order to make the change.

Some dry cleaners will pick up and drop off your cleaning. You can order almost anything online now, so there is no need to spend time actually visiting the supermarket or physically shopping, therefore, I suggest you do as much as you can online. You could arrange to car share with other parents for after school activities or even the journey to and from school.

By taking a good look at all the areas where you're spending your time and finding creative ways to maximise its usage, you'll be amazed how much time you're actually able to free up. Every client who has completed this exercise has been able to free up a substantial amount of time enabling him or her to schedule more value added activities and 'Me Time'.

The following is a list of the things that you could do to save time and to be more organised. Being more organised gives you time back because it allows you to complete tasks in a logical order:

- Get someone to do mundane tasks such as ironing/gardening/cleaning/car valeting.

- Get your dry cleaning collected.

- Car share the school journey and after school activities with other parents.

- Get a virtual PA - if you have a very hectic life, it may be worth investing in a virtual PA, someone who will do all the day to day 'running around' for you e.g. booking holidays or making travel arrangements, paying your bills, making appointments etc you can find a virtual PA very easily online - remember to take up references.

- Automate your bill paying - set up standing orders and Direct Debits wherever possible so that you don't have to remember to pay bills.

- Do your banking online (if you don't already) - I know so many people who are still trudging to their local bank branch in order to manage their account which is totally unnecessary now that everything can be done online or via telephone and it's completely safe.

- Stop watching so much TV!

- Look for areas where you can do two things at once e.g. if you drive a lot, use your journeys to make calls (safely) or listen to an e-book or self-help programme.

- Order as much as you can on-line.

- Review all the after school clubs that your children attend - are they really necessary and are they benefitting your child - do they really enjoy them or are they going because *you* think they *should?*

- Make 'To Do Lists' - *what gets written down gets done* - get everything out of your head and onto paper, crossing off each activity when it has been completed. I write a new 'To Do List' at the end of each day, carrying forward anything that I've not completed that day, making it a priority for the next.

- Always do the things that you don't want to do first - often

193

we can spend more time worrying about doing something or worrying that we haven't done it, than the time it would take to do it.

- Make batches of food for dinner and freeze it rather than cooking from scratch each meal or eating readymade supermarket food.

This list is by no means exhaustive. When you've done your time audit, look at the areas where you're not making best use of your time and replace those activities with more value-added ones. Again, think about how much your time costs in monetary terms versus how much it would cost to bring someone else in. If you're a high earner, it's an obvious choice. However, even if you aren't, it may still make sense for you if it gives you time back that could be used in a more productive way or gives you more time with your family – it's difficult to put a price on that.

KEY LEARNING POINTS

1. OUR BODY LANGUAGE AFFECTS OUR THOUGHTS

- Our physiology and our emotions are inextricably linked.

- If you want to change your feelings quickly, change your physiology and emulate the body language and facial expressions of the emotion that you *want* to feel.

- Do the Superhero stance for 2 minutes to change your biochemistry quickly and feel more powerful and in control.

2. THE POWER OF WORDS

- Our words have power - we experience the emotions attached to the words that we use i.e. if we use strong words we're likely to experience strong emotions associated with that word.

- If we don't use a word, we aren't likely to experience that associated emotion or feeling.

- Our brains do not recognise the word 'don't', therefore, you should construct sentences in positive terms rather than using the word 'don't' i.e. "carry that carefully" instead of "don't drop that".

- Stop using the words *'ought'*, *'should'*, *'must'* - they lead to procrastination and being judgmental when used in reference to others.

3. THE POWER OF VISUALISATION

- *The mind can't tell the difference between something real and something vividly imagined.*

- Practise visualising what you do want rather than what you don't.

- Practise visualising positive outcomes for potentially stressful situations. See them in as much detail as possible, see what you would see, hear what you would hear and feel what you would feel if everything were to go perfectly.

- Visualising a positive outcome greatly increases your chances of success.

4. RELAXATION TECHNIQUES

- Learn and use relaxation techniques to help you gain more control in stressful situations.

- The more time you practise the techniques, the quicker and easier it will become to feel relaxed as you create and deepen neural pathways.

- Deep breathing releases endorphins and helps combat high levels of the stress hormone cortisol.

5. STOP UNHELPFUL SLEEP PATTERNS

- We often wake up in the middle of the night worrying about something that our subconscious has not been able to satisfactorily process.

- Keep a notepad and pen by the side of the bed and note down any thoughts that wake you in the night - that will often be enough for the subconscious to consider the matter dealt with and it's likely that you'll go straight back to sleep.

- Alter your bed time and go to bed and wake up at the same time (even at weekends) for two weeks in order to establish a sound sleeping pattern.

6. THE POWER OF EXERCISE

- Exercise is important not simply because it keeps us fit and healthy, but changes our biochemistry by releasing endorphins which help deal with stress-related hormones that may be present if we've been experiencing consistent stress or anxiety.

- Schedule exercise in your diary as you would any other

important, immoveable meeting or diary appointment.

- When you exercise on a consistent basis, the healthier and more in control you'll feel.

7. SCHEDULE 'ME TIME'

- It's important that no matter how busy your life is that you schedule 'Me Time', time for you do something that makes you happier and healthier.

- 'Me Time' must be scheduled in your diary and must be immovable.

- If you're unhappy, anxious and stressed, that's how you're teaching your kids to be.

- Do a Time Audit and see where you're spending your time and where it can be utilised to better effect.

- Outsource as many activities as possible and use online options for shopping and paying bills.

- Being more organised will free up time, enabling you to do more added value activities - get into the habit of creating daily 'To do Lists'.

CHAPTER 6

"Your happiness is right inside you right now"

VICTIM OR OWNER?

Are you a victim or an owner? In other words, do you class yourself as lucky or unlucky, positive or negative, happy or unhappy? Most people fall into one category or the other and as *we have to remain consistent with our view of ourselves* we completely associate with that view and think and behave in a way that consistently fulfils it.

There have been numerous studies on this subject and the overwhelming evidence shows that the results achieved by people who consider themselves to be lucky are happier, healthier and overall wealthier than their 'unlucky' counterparts. However, those people are actually not any luckier, the same negative situations happen to them as they do to unlucky people. The difference is they *choose* (either consciously or unconsciously) to view situations differently. They have a different *perception* or perspective which makes them more resourceful, allowing them to make better decisions and take consistent action.

Let's look at the difference between Victims and Owners:

VICTIMS...

- Class themselves as unlucky and tend to frequently tell people how unlucky they are.

- Continually moan about their situation but rarely do anything about it.

- Take little or no responsibility for their situation - everything is someone or something else's fault.

- Feel sorry for themselves and are self pitying.

- Frequently participate in gossip.

- Display negative body language and speak negatively almost continuously.

- When things are going right, they wait for it to go wrong or say things like, "It won't last" or "It's bound to go wrong, this is too good to last".

- Believe that nothing good ever happens to them.

- Are 'glass half empty'.

- Have a strong inner critic.

- Ask themselves disempowering questions e.g. "Why me?"

A friend of mine has a name for extreme Victims; she calls them 'Mood Hoovers' because she says they literally suck the positivity out of those around them. They also tend to gravitate toward positive people; they seem feed off their positive energy. They usually have a good old moan to the positive person who will often try to help them. However, they Victim doesn't actually want help, they are attention seeking (that tends to be the main secondary gain for their behaviour). At the end of the moan, they will go off perfectly happy, leaving the positive person (if they don't protect themselves against it) feeling deflated, drained and potential in a negative state.

The problem with this is that eventually no-one will want to listen to their continual moaning, especially when the Victim doesn't seem to make any effort to change things. This can be exasperating especially if they are moaning to a person in the 'Owner' category who will start to find ways to avoid the Victim altogether.

OWNERS

Owners are, as you would imagine, the exact opposite of a Victim and they...

- Take responsibility for their lives.

- Take control of and deal with issues in a positive way.

- Bounce back from problems quickly, if they fail, they get up and try again.

- Consider themselves to be lucky.

- Don't take "no" for an answer.

- Look for the positives in a situation.

- Don't dwell on the negative.

- Look for opportunities.

- Don't think too much about what other people think of them.

- Are 'glass half full'.

- **Ask empowering questions**, e.g. "What can I do about this?"

A popular misconception that Victims make is that Owners don't have the same problems as they do, that somehow Owners are miraculously shielded by a superhero cape that protects them from negative situations. That is utter rubbish! Exactly the same illnesses, money issues, family problems, floods, fires, job/business losses, births, marriages and deaths happen to Owners as they do Victims. The difference is how they *think* and *feel* about what's happening to them. **Owners *choose* (consciously or subconsciously) to think positively about their life and the situations that arise.** That's it – that's all there is – that's the difference.

Owners are no luckier than Victims; they simply choose to see things in a more positive way and because they have that positive view, they are ultimately much more resourceful. Their mind isn't clouded by doubt, sadness, apathy, negativity and therefore they see things more clearly and are able to take positive action. They view situations without negative emotions, which enables them to deal with things more effectively.

When I have this conversation with my less positive clients, the first thing they usually say is, "It's alright for you, you're a positive person, but I can't do that". Well I'm living proof that anyone can change, as I said at the beginning of the book, I haven't always lived with a positive outlook. It is possible to think more positively and move from being a Victim to an Owner, even if you've had a lifetime of negative thoughts, you always have a choice. I'm not saying that you should be positive every second of every day, that would be unrealistic, but what I will say is that if you notice any negativity creeping in, you can deal with it quickly before it takes a hold, using the techniques I've described in this book.

DOES YOUR NEGATIVITY DEFINE YOU?

Do you know someone who is constantly/consistently negative? They see nothing positive or good in their lives; they obsess about how awful their job is, how their friend has let them down, how they have no money, how everything in their life goes wrong etc. They identify with their negativity so much that it seems to become who they are.

Alternatively, have you ever met someone who seems to revel (in a very unhealthy way) in an illness that they have? They can't wait to tell you every tiny detail of the illness, what happened at their latest doctors/hospital appointment, what treatment has been prescribed and how much it's negatively affecting their lives. Again, they identify so closely with their illness that it almost becomes who they are.

So why do they do it? With most people, it will almost certainly be classic attention seeking, usually through a subconscious need to be loved and listened to - their dramatic tales of woe getting and keeping them in the limelight. All the focus is on them when they tell their story and are told, "Oh how awful for you" "Hang in there you'll be fine" "Oh I'm so sorry, how are you coping?" It also feeds the Victim persona really rather well and makes them feel significant.

HOW OTHER PEOPLE'S NEGATIVITY CAN AFFECT YOU

We need to be conscious when we're around very negative people so that we aren't influenced by their negative behaviour; it can be really easy to get dragged into a *'my life is worse than yours'* competition. My advice would be to limit the amount of time you spend with overly negative people and when you do come across them, try to bring the conversation back to something positive. I know that can be particularly difficult if you work or live with that type of person. I'm often asked to coach a particularly negative team member who is affecting (or infecting) the whole team with their negativity, so I know what a detrimental it can have.

You may even recognise yourself here, either as someone who talks a lot about their illness/is consistently negative or as someone who gets in a battle about whose illness/life is worse. We learn to do that in the playground - do you remember the arguments we had as children where the kid that could end with "Well my dad's a policeman!" was the winner?

If you identify with any of these personality traits and are guilty of displaying them, here are some practical things you can do to overcome them:

- Give yourself a pat on the back for recognising it! As I've explained previously, acknowledging emotions and behaviours is often enough for us to make the necessary conscious and subconscious adjustments needed to change.

- We get more of what we think about, therefore constantly thinking, dwelling, talking, identifying with an illness or viewing everything as negative brings more illness or negativity to you. You therefore need to get into the habit of noticing those negative thoughts and change them before you get into a negative spiral (we covered how to change your thoughts in Chapter 4).

- Change your response - when someone asks you how you are stop and think about how you want to reply. What you need to know is that PEOPLE DON'T WANT TO HEAR NOR DO THEY EXPECT TO HEAR THE INS AND OUTS OF YOUR PROBLEMS, THEY ARE GENERALLY ASKING OUT OF POLITENESS. Whilst I'm sure *some* do genuinely care, no-one is looking for a detailed response to that question and you'll be turning them off by launching into a whole tirade about how bad things are and ultimately you may find they start to avoid you.

Here are some responses that you may want to adopt to replace your old 'moaning':

- "It's been tough but I'm getting there."

- "My mind's great and my body is close behind."

- "Getting better every day."

- "I'm brilliant, thanks!"

My personal favourite is "I'm fabulous, thanks!" I use this almost every time someone asks me how I am. I've said it so many times over the years that it's now become an automatic response and I really do mean it!

Remember what we discussed in the last Chapter about the importance of carefully choosing the words you use, you can't get the feeling if you don't use the word. In addition, if you use positive words you're much more likely to use positive physiology which will directly affect your emotions and make you feel better instantly.

No matter how hard or tempting it may be to start your 'woe is me story', resist with all your might. Don't be drawn into the detailed negativity of what's happening – smile, thank them for asking and move on to talking about things that are more positive. The more you practise this, the easier it will become and the more people will want to be around you. If you do find yourself launching into your 'story', stop yourself and say, "...but I'm feeling much better, thanks" or "...but things are getting better, thanks".

THE SECONDARY GAIN OF A VICTIM

As I mentioned earlier, Victims are simply looking for attention and will have found growing up that either having an illness or consistently being negative got them attention. However, that behaviour won't serve them in the same way as adults. If you identify with this, you need to find a more constructive way to get the attention you need. Do something lovely and unexpected for your friends or family. It could be something as simple as baking a cake, cooking a meal, taking your child to the park, calling a friend you've not seen for a while and listening to them for a change. That will get you positive attention and they will love you even more for it.

Now I've pointed these things out, you'll probably notice them whether it's you doing them or others. If you find yourself in a conversation with someone who is being negative, and you can't seem to steer them back to something positive then you need to try listening with passivity - literally taking a step back in your mind's eye is a good way to disassociate yourself from what they are saying. They are their issues not yours, therefore, avoid trying to solve their problems for them – they usually don't want help anyway, they just want attention. Make sure that when you finish talking to them you immediately put yourself back in a more positive state. Think positive thoughts, think of someone or something you love in order to stop their negativity from rubbing off on you.

ASK BETTER QUESTIONS

One of the big differences between Victims and Owners is the questions that they ask themselves. In essence, Owners ask empowering questions such as:

- "How can I use this?"

- "What can I do to get around this?"

- "What can I learn from this?"

Whereas the Victim asks disempowering questions like:

- Why me?

- Why am I so unlucky?

- Why does this keep happening to me?

Whether you realise it or not, *you have the answers to your issues/problems/dilemmas within you*. Therefore, the quality of the questions you ask yourself is so important, as you have the power to turn your situations from negative to positive and vice versa through your questioning process.

Your brain is designed to answer every single question you ask of it, troubles tend occur when we ask ourselves poor questions; *ask a poor question, get a poor answer.* Here are some disempowering questions that are likely to give a negative response if you ask them of yourself:

Q. "Why can't I lose weight"

A. "Because I'm fat and lazy"

Q. "Why does this always happen to me?"

A. "Because I'm unlucky and it sums my life up"

Q. "Why does nothing ever work out right?"

A. "Because nothing good ever happens to me"

Q. "Why can't I ever seem to get a break?"

A. "Because I'm a failure"

Whatever questions we ask of ourselves, we will get an answer – whether we like the answer or not. It's therefore important not only to ask good quality questions, but that we state them in the positive e.g.:

- "What can I do to change this?"

- "What actions can I take to solve this?"

- "What else could this mean?"

- "What can I learn from this?"

- "How can I use what I've learnt?"

- "How can I turn this into an opportunity?"

If you consistently learn to use this positive style of questioning, it's likely that you'll find solutions to your problems more quickly and easily than if you ask poor/disempowering 'pity party' questions.

It seems incredibly simplistic, and it is. Listen to the types of questions you ask yourself, I can guarantee that if you're a negative person you'll be asking negative questions and getting unhelpful, often self-pitying responses.

If you're aware that you ask yourself unhelpful questions, it may be useful to write down some more empowering ones (the ones above are a good start) and keep them somewhere accessible so that you can start to break your old negative questioning habits and replace them with more useful ones.

After reading this section if you recognise yourself as Victim, it's within your control to change. You simply have to choose to take charge of your thinking and the questions you ask yourself. It just takes practise to change those old neural pathways and replace them with new ones.

WHAT'S YOUR STORY?

Our storytelling generates powerful emotions within us; our story is usually the explanation we use to justify why we don't have what we want in our lives right now or why is it like it is. Our stories are our excuses for not having achieved what we thought or expected that we would have done by this time in our lives.

The following list demonstrates some of excuses we tend use for not having achieved what we hoped we would:

- *Upbringing* - "My parents never supported me" "My parents were negative" "I wasn't allowed to do or try things growing up".

- *Education or lack of education* - This is an interesting one, I know of at least half a dozen entrepreneurs (Simon Cowell

212

included) who don't have any formal qualifications and they have not let their lack of education stop them.

- *Lack of role models growing up* - "Nobody really succeeds in our family".

- *Children* - "I need to look after my children and their happiness comes first" - What about your happiness? Would you be different around them if you were happier? Would they be happier if you were?

- *Partner* - "My partner doesn't support me" "He/she says I should stick to what I'm doing now and don't take the risk"

- *People like me...* - "People like me just don't do that", "It's OK for other people..." They're just excuses, plain and simple.

- *Lack of time* - If you really wanted something badly enough, you would make time. Do a time audit (see Chapter 5) actually write down everything you do in a week from hour to hour and you'll be amazed how much time you waste.

- *Lack of money* - Often when I work with clients who have this excuse for not reaching their goal, I ask them to list everything they need spend money on to achieve the goal or at least to get started (that makes it more real), quite often they find it's far less than what they had anticipated.

Going right back to the first chapter when we talked about taking responsibility for our lives, is it really something or someone else's fault when we underachieve or don't reach our goals or are we simply relinquishing responsibility and using excuses? If, after asking yourself that question you still think it is someone else's fault, then ask yourself what evidence you have to support your argument. If you can't think of any tangible reasons, then you're just making excuses and not taking responsibility.

WHO WOULD YOU BE WITHOUT YOUR STORY?

What's *your* story? What story have you been using to make you feel better about what you don't have in your life right now? **Who would you be, what would you have, what would you be doing if you didn't have that story holding you back?**

Take a good look at the stories you've been telling yourself and create a new, more empowering one. Now is the time to let go of all of those old excuses. Once you have your new story, visualise it in as much detail as possible and think about it often. By doing that you'll be creating new neural pathways that will make that new, compelling story much more real and achievable - *thoughts become things*. Changing almost anything is within your power and only you can make your life better - stop waiting for someone or something else to change it for you or to rescue you. You simply need to DECIDE, draw up a workable PLAN and TAKE ACTION NOW!

RID YOURSELF OF FEAR & WORRY

We all get fearful from time to time, but what is fear? In this day and age is there anything we really need to fear? After all, we're hardly likely to be eaten by a sabre-toothed tiger or trampled by a herd of woolly mammoths. The fear that our distant ancestors faced due to being in constant life-threatening situations was very different to the fear we feel now. However, those same feelings haven't yet evolved out of us; we still have them whether we're actually in danger or whether we're just imagining the worst case scenario.

For the purposes of this book, I'm not talking about the fear you may experience when you're walking home late at night on your own – that is REAL fear and you've every right to feel fearful, it's that fear that keeps us safe. What I am talking about is imagined fear, the scenarios we run through in our minds that drive us to distraction inducing feelings of pain and worry. Those feelings of fear, we **DO** have control over, as they are thoughts generated by us. After all, those awful things that we're vividly imagining haven't actually happened. However, they do elicit strong emotions which makes the scenario 'feel' very real. That's because *our minds can't tell the difference between something that's real and something that's vividly imagined* (I make no apologies for saying that repeatedly!).

Here's an example which illustrates this idea perfectly. A couple of months ago, I recognised that I had started to become fearful that something I had been working hard on might not come to fruition, which would adversely affect me financially. I noticed that I was becoming more and more fearful as I ran scenarios of what would happen if it didn't work out. In a very short space of time, those negative thoughts had spiralled and I ended up in my mind, bankrupt and out on the streets with nowhere to live within a matter of months. I started to have sleepless nights (something I've not suffered from for a very long time) and I had let my fear take away my reasoning, my control and my confidence.

Then one day, completely unexpectedly I woke up and thought, "I'm tired of feeling like this. I'm not doing it anymore," I literally stopped worrying, just like that and I've not worried about it since. Although from time to time I do get a little negative niggle because after you've had a particular thought for a while, you'll have created quite a strong neural pathway which means it can manifest itself again quickly and easily when you least expect it if you don't consciously stop it. However, if that thought does come I just ignore it, wave it away and do something more constructive immediately, before it gets the chance to grab a hold and spiral.

At the point of writing this book, the issue I was fearful about is still not yet resolved, however, I'm not fearful about the outcome. Because of that, I can think and plan with more clarity and more effectiveness now that I'm no longer running those unhelpful images, triggering negative emotions pulling me into learnt helplessness.

You may think that it's not possible or as simple to stop worrying as I have indicated. You may even think, "Well, it's alright for you but I can't do that" but, you can, everyone can. You generate your thoughts, so you can change them. You simply have to recognise that you're having those fearful, negative thoughts (and that's all they are, thoughts, generated by you) and change them to something more positive.

GET A PLAN

One way to help deal with real issues that could potentially have a negative outcome is to think about them logically as soon as you recognise that there may be a problem. Work them through, looking at all the possibilities and come up with a solution even for the worst-case scenario. Having a plan and facing the issue head on will give you back control and help you manage the issue effectively.

Another helpful tool in managing fear is taking whatever you're worrying about and visualising a perfect outcome, the outcome you really want. By focussing on a positive outcome, you're much more likely to get it which will also help you to feel more positive and resourceful.

Some statistics that I recently read indicated that 90% of what we fear never happens. If you're a negative person, you're likely to say, "Well 10% could go wrong", yes, 10% could go wrong, but if you have a plan for the 90% then you'll easily be able to handle the 10%.

It would be remiss of me not to point out here that sometimes a little 'controlled' fear can be good for us. Footballers, actors, public speakers and musicians all say that they experience some fear before they perform, but it's a good fear. It's usually caused by a shot of adrenalin that helps us focus and deliver an excellent performance. That adrenaline shot again comes from our ancestors 'fight or flight' response.

In summary, being fearful and worrying unnecessarily is rarely useful unless you do find yourself in real physical danger. Fear comes from thoughts of what *could* happen which is usually not based on reality. Take action and plan for worst-case scenarios where you can, then let them go - train yourself to think of something positive, after all, we can't have two thoughts at once.

"Change your thoughts, change your world"

DEALING WITH SELF-SABOTAGE

Have you ever thought that you may be sabotaging your own goals? You get so far with something and then do or say something and it all falls apart? I don't think there's anyone alive who hasn't. Sometimes clients tell me that they know that they're self-sabotaging but really don't know why.

Self-sabotage is like misguided self-love. If you self-sabotage, there's some part of you (usually deep in your subconscious) that is in conflict with what you're trying to consciously achieve. Your subconscious is actively protecting you from something that it *perceives* to be harmful or not in your best interest.

OVERCOMING SELF-SABOTAGE

To overcome self-sabotage, firstly, take a good look at your goals. Are they what I call authentic goals i.e. something that you really want, or are they something that you *think* you should want/have? Are they *your* goals or the goals of your parents, spouse or friends? What you may find when you dig deep is that there's a conflict between what you *think* you want (or what you think you *should* want) and what you *really* want. If that is the case, no matter how hard you try to achieve your goal, your subconscious will go about ensuring that it doesn't happen.

If you're happy that your goal is authentic but you still find that you sabotage your efforts, it could be that what you desire is in direct conflict to what you actually think that you can have or achieve. This conflict will be enough for your subconscious to actively go about sabotaging your efforts. This can also be true if you think that you aren't worthy of your goal.

I notice this particularly when it comes to the subject of money. Clients want more money, but often have such negative associations with it that they either self-sabotage on the way to getting it or when they have it, often resulting in them losing a good chunk, if not all of it. Often the negative associations come from unresolved money issues such as hearing our parents say things like "Only bad people make money" "Money is the root of all evil" or "Money doesn't grow on trees". It's no wonder that we self-sabotage, when we're running that type of subconscious programming. Do you use these types of statements? If so, be careful if you say them around your children as you'll be programming them with the same limiting thoughts and beliefs that you have.

Another common internal conflict area is a new job or

promotion. Many people dearly want to move up the ladder and gain a coveted promotion or get the job of their dreams; however, they mess up the interview (even when they have done all the preparation humanly possible). When this happens, I ask particularly probing questions and usually uncover that the client doesn't actually believe that they can get/do the job or they think they aren't worthy of it. Recognising and removing those conflicts usually results in achieving their goals more quickly than they could have imagined as their conscious and subconscious thoughts are then aligned.

What we have to remember is that there is a reason for everything we (or others) do, whether we realise what that is or not, there's always a secondary gain. The next time you find yourself self-sabotaging, ask yourself some empowering questions such as:

- "Why do I want this?" Getting clear about the reasons for wanting something is very important – if the 'why' is not big or strong enough, it's unlikely that you'll achieve your goal.

- "What's the meaning/message in this?"

- "What's REALLY stopping me?" If you think you don't know what's stopping you, ask the question "If I *did* know what would it be?" This is a very powerful question that changes the emphasis and often helps you come to quicker conclusions.

- "What can I do about it?"

- "Is this the right goal for me, at this time?"

- "Is this goal really mine, or is it someone else's?"

- "Do I *really* want this or do I want it because I *think* I should or someone else wants me to have it?"

Asking yourself probing, quality questions will enable you to uncover what is really stopping you. Once you've established that, you then have options:

- Drop the goal completely.

- Revise the goal to something more compelling.

- Devise a SMART (Specific, Measurable, Attainable, Realistic, Time-bound) plan for how you're going to reach your goal.

BE HAPPY NOW!

There seems to be an epidemic that people think that they are going be happy "**when**"...

- "... I get my new house."

- "... I get my new car."

- "... I find a husband/wife."

- "... I get a new job."

- "... My children go to university."

- "... I'm earning more money."

- "... I can afford to go on holiday/get that new sofa/get a new kitchen/finish the house/buy what I want."

Your happiness does not depend on anything external. *Your happiness is right inside, you right now*; you just need to recognise it. What happens when we think, "I'll be happy when..." is that we project our happiness into the future. When we're focused on the future, we aren't able to enjoy what is happening now.

When we project our happiness into the future we create strong neural pathways, conditioning our minds to believe that happiness is always in the future. So when you actually do get that new house/car/husband/wife/partner/child, your mind still believes that happiness is in the future and so your 'happiness goals' change, "I'll be happy when I get a second house in the country/a bigger car/two cars/an even better job" etc.

Look back at the things you have now that at one point you thought would make you happy if you had them. Did they make you happy? If they did, how long was it before you were looking for the next thing to replace it?

You'd be surprised how many unhappy/depressed millionaires there are out there. You hear in the press all the time about this or that millionaire film star/musician/athlete suffering from depression or ending up in rehab for one reason or another. They have every material thing they could ever wish for and yet they're still unhappy. That's because they're looking for happiness outside themselves.

HAPPINESS COMES FROM WITHIN

So how do we find our happiness right now? Stop and look around you, look at the good things you have in your life right now and BE GRATEFUL for what you do have. Get into the habit of thinking about them, giving thanks for them and loving them. Gratitude is so important and makes such a difference. Once we actually sit back and take time out to be grateful for what we have - and we all have something that we're grateful for - it puts us in a much more positive state which affects everything.

When I talk about this with my more negative clients, this is usually how the conversation goes:

Client: "There's nothing good in my life, everything's awful, and I've got nothing to be happy about."

Me: "Really? So you don't love your children? You're not happy and grateful that you've got them?"

Client: "Well, yeah, of course, but..."

Me: "So you don't like your house/your parents/your friends and you didn't like the holiday you've just been on?"

Client: "Well yeah, of course I do/did, but..."

Me: "So you don't like good weather/socialising with loved ones/walking in the country/your hobbies?"

Client: "Well I suppose I do, but ..."

Me: "But you've just said there's nothing good in your life and nothing to be happy about!"

Client: "Well I haven't got enough money/time/qualifications..."

Me: "OK, but you do have good things in your life that you're happy about?"

Client: "Yes, I suppose I do!"

What I then do is get my client to think about all the things that they love and are grateful for. I do this exercise with them:

EXERCISE 21

BE GRATEFUL, VISUALISE

Make a list of as many things as possible that you love and that you're grateful for.

Once you have your list, clearly visualise those things in your mind:

1. Make the pictures big, bright and colourful.

2. Add sound.

3. Feel all the good feelings you have when you think about those things.

4. If you have a still picture, make it into a movie.

5. Add as many of those mini movies together and play them as many times as possible until it's easy to see it in detail, hearing what you would hear, feeling what you would feel and seeing what you would see. Replay each of your mini movies back-to-back, over and over again.

Repeat this exercise as many times as you can during the day (especially when negative thoughts appear – it's a wonderful technique for removing them). When you do this and it only takes a couple of minutes, you'll start to feel good instantly. Two things happen when you do this exercise:

1. When you repeatedly play your positive/happy movies, you'll automatically create the good feelings that go with the thoughts, positively which will affect your behaviour.

2. You create new neural pathways that associate feeling good and feeling happy NOW instead of sometime in the future (that never comes).

You can play these movies at any time and they will always increase your feelings of well-being and happiness.

Another tool that I ask my clients to use is to create a Gratitude Journal. Each evening they write down five things that they are grateful for. They have to be five things that happened that day not just regular things that they're always grateful for like, kids, family, husband, wife etc. By doing this, they start to train their minds to look out for the good, positive things that they've experienced during each day. Just completing this simple exercise on a daily basis can increase your positivity levels immeasurably.

KEY LEARNING POINTS

1. VICTIM OR OWNER

- Are you a Victim? Victims blame everyone else for their misfortune and take no responsibility for their lives, ask themselves disempowering questions and consider themselves unlucky - they often live in learnt helplessness.

- Are you an Owner? Owners take responsibility, they realise that bad things happen but they *decide* to think positively, ask great questions and take positive action.

- You can actively choose whether you want to be a Victim or an Owner (lucky or unlucky, positive or negative) - it's a decision, it's how you think and how you behave that makes you a Victim or an Owner.

- Owners have been proven to be more successful and happier than those who perceive themselves to be a Victim/unlucky.

2. ASK BETTER QUESTIONS

- The quality of our questions affects the quality of our lives.

- Our brains are designed to answer any question we ask of it, if we ask lousy questions, we get lousy answers.

- Learn to ask yourself better questions like: "How can I use this?" - "What can I do differently?" - "What do I need to do to stop this happening again?"

3. WHAT'S YOUR STORY?

- What story have you been telling yourself about why you haven't achieved your goals? Is that story true? How do you know it's true?

- Who would you be without your story? If your story is no longer serving you, replace it with something more compelling and empowering.

4. RID YOURSELF OF FEAR & WORRY

- We experience fear and worry as a result of the images that we create in our minds, therefore, if we don't create the pictures or the thoughts we won't have the feelings.

- If you're worrying about something, take some time out to really look at the problem and draw up a plan of action.

- If there's no action or planning that you can do, practise letting the thoughts go and visualising the outcome that you want; a positive outcome.

5. DEALING WITH SELF-SABOTAGE

- We often self-sabotage when the goal we're trying to achieve isn't one that we really want e.g. it is no longer relevant, it's something that we *think* we should want or it's something that someone else thinks we should want/have.

- Ask yourself some positive, empowering questions to ascertain whether the goal is an authentic one and drop it if it's not.

- Set yourself some new goals using the SMART format (Specific, Measurable, Attainable, Realistic, Time bound) and make sure that you decide to take at least one action towards its attainment the same day as you set your goal to get momentum going.

6. BE HAPPY NOW!

- Happiness comes from within - no amount of 'stuff' will make you happy.

- By projecting your happiness into the future e.g. if you often say, "I'll be happy when..." you're training your brain to think that happiness will always be in the future and never now.

- Unfortunately, by training our brains that way, when we do attain the 'things' we've been coveting, our brain still thinks that happiness is in the future and we aren't satisfied for long.

- Learn to practise Gratitude - the more grateful we are the happier we become.

- Start a Gratitude Journal each evening, write five new things that you're grateful for that happened during that day - by doing this you'll be looking back through the day finding the good things that have happened and training your brain to be happy and grateful now rather than sometime in the future.

Visit www.thoughtsbecomethings.co.uk for a Gratitude template that you can use daily to capture the things you're grateful for.

JO BANKS

WHAT NEXT?

"You get more of what you think about"

We've finally come to the end of the book and now it's up to you to put take action. Only you can make the changes necessary to have a fabulous life, it's completely within your control. **With only small but consistent changes, you can make a massive positive difference to your life.**

As a recap, the following are what I consider the most important points for you to learn and put into practice from this book, even if you did nothing else but get into the habit of using these techniques daily, it would build new strong neural pathways making your life much more positive and happy. They really don't take much effort or time but will have a huge impact if used consistently (it has been scientifically proven that if we practise anything for 21 days, it becomes a habit):

233

1. *Take responsibility*

   Take responsibility for everything you have in your life - you've created it and it's in your power to change it, stop blaming others or waiting for someone/something to rescue you.

2. *Secondary gain*

   Look for the secondary gain you've been getting for any behaviour you want to change - once you've identified that, it will be easier for you to adjust your behaviour so that you get the gain you want but in a more appropriate way.

3. *Change your thoughts*

   YOU create your thoughts; therefore, if you don't like what you've been thinking, CHANGE IT! Your thoughts are completely within your control - change your negative ones as soon as you notice them, don't let them spiral out of control - shout, "STOP", simply wave them on or use an elastic band to remind yourself to change them.

4. *Change your physiology*

   If you want to change your emotions quickly, change your physiology (body language), go for a walk (*motion creates emotion*) or simply *do* something different.

5. *Choose your words*

The words we use are very powerful; if you don't use a word, you aren't likely to experience the emotion associated it. Remember to make statements that are in the positive and avoid using the word 'don't' as the brain doesn't recognise it. Also avoid using *'must', 'ought' and 'should'* – it's the language of procrastination and is judgmental when used in reference to others.

6. *Visualise what you want*

Create clear, precise, colourful, noisy pictures or videos of how you want things to be - feel what you would feel, hear what you would hear and see what you would see. Practise visualising as many times as possible so that you create a deep neural pathway that convinces the subconscious that it has already been achieved - this is a great technique to calm interview or presentation nerves and to actually get what you want.

7. *Choose how you perceive a situation*

Your perception becomes your reality, nothing is real. It's the meaning that you put to something that makes it positive or negative/good or bad. Get into the habit of questioning your perception ask yourself, "How do I know this?" "What evidence do I have to support my view?" "What else could this mean?"

8. *Victim or Owner*

Choose to be an Owner, like anything else, it is a choice, it's not pre-destined. Owners are proven to be happier, healthier and more successful, they don't have fewer problems than Victims, they simply choose to see things differently. They ask better questions and take decisive action until they achieve positive results.

9. *The past doesn't equal the future/Your story*

Just because something negative happened to you in the past doesn't mean that it will happen to you again. Look at the stories that you've been telling yourself about why you haven't succeeded and ask yourself, "Who would I be without that story?" Let go of any stories that aren't beneficial and that are holding you back.

10. *Be happy now!*

Happiness is internal; it comes from within you and not from what happens to you or from other people/possessions. Stop waiting for someone else to change things or rescue you. Stop waiting for something to happen to you in order to be happy e.g. "I'll be happy when..." If you keep doing that, you're training your mind to think that happiness is dependent on something external to you and that it's always in the future. Practising daily gratitude will help you to get into the habit of looking for the positives. The more you do that, the happier and more positive your life will become.

AND FINALLY...

Make the decision to be one of the few that actually puts into practice what they read and you too can experience the positive changes in your life that my clients and I have experienced. The key to living an exceptional, happy life is to keep trying and never give up. There may be days when you 'forget' to apply the methods I've described, however, the key here is to not get disheartened but to try again as soon as you become aware of it.

The great thing about life is every day we get the chance to start again. Start to question your old programming or that critical inner voice and make a concerted effort to change your thoughts and behaviours to ones that serve you – it's totally within your power.

GOOD LUCK!

All that leaves me now is to wish you the very best of luck (remember that we make our own luck ... it's a choice). I truly hope that you've enjoyed this book and make some remarkable changes in your life as a result of reading it and applying what you've learnt. Please remember to pass onto others what has worked for you - it's always good to pay it forward!

ADDITIONAL RESOURCES

Visit the website and sign up with a quality email address for free access to a range of templates and information that work hand-in-hand with this book, specifically designed to help facilitate long-lasting change.

www.thoughtsbecomethings.co.uk

For more information on the services that Jo's business, What Next Consultancy, provides (including 1:2:1 transformational coaching with Jo herself) and to read testimonials about how her coaching has helped her clients, visit:

www.whatnextconsultancy.co.uk

You can also sign up for the What Next Newsletter, a monthly email which includes hints and tips for leading a healthier, more productive and happier life. You can also keep up-to-date with Jo's most recent tips and advice by reading her blog at:

www.whatnextconsultancy.co.uk/blog

JO BANKS

REFERENCE LINKS

Dane Brookes http://groupdane.com/

Tony Robbins https://www.tonyrobbins.com/

Paul McKenna http://www.paulmckenna.com/

Richard Bandler http://richardbandler.com/

Michael Neil http://www.supercoach.com/

Robert Holden http://www.robertholden.org/

JK Rowling http://www.jkrowling.com/

Jack Canfield http://jackcanfield.com/

Sylvester Stallone http://sylvesterstallone.com/

Duncan Ballantyne https://www.bannatyne.co.uk/about-duncan/

Sir Richard Branson http://www.virgin.com/richard-branson

Mark Victor Hansen http://markvictorhansen.com/

JO BANKS

ACKNOWLEDGMENTS

Firstly, I'd like to thank my long suffering friends who have stood by me through thick and thin and who have always been there to support me, no matter what – Michelle Kirby ("More Prosecco please") and the gorgeous Kirby Family, Justine Williams ("Our Champagne Saturdays are the stuff of legend"), Sharon Cunningham ("They're just mood Hoovers!") and Jo Cranham ("I'm in Barbados counting my winnings!"). I love you ladies, you ROCK!

Next, I have to thank my fabulous web designer, business owner, author and friend, Dane Brookes. His help and advice on the technical aspects of book publishing have been invaluable, not to mention the design of the book cover and fabulous, innovative websites that his company (http://groupdane.com) have created for me. I'd have struggled and it would have been a much more painful process if it were not for his help and guidance.

I'd like to express my gratitude to Kevin Parks, Debbie Hinbest, Lyndsay Chambers and Diane Hall for your continued faith and trust in my abilities. My business would not be where it is today without your support.

Also fully deserving of my thanks are Nisha Srivastava, Wendy Dolan, Joanne Griffiths and Lynn Sefton – thank you all for your continued support ladies. You make me laugh, keep me sane and always provide a friendly ear whenever I'm in need. I appreciate it more than I can say.

I'd also like to thank the many clients past and present, without your support and trust, this would all be theory.

Finally, I'd like to thank my dad, my rock. No matter what happens he is always there for me unconditionally, supporting me and providing his invaluable insights. I love you dad.

ABOUT THE AUTHOR

Jo Banks, a Business Owner, Transformational Coach, NLP Master Practitioner and CBT Therapist has more than 20 years experience as a Senior HR Professional, establishing her own Coaching and Consultancy Practice, What Next Consultancy (UK) Ltd in 2009. With experience of working within a range of industries, Jo has a strong track record in positively creating high-performance cultures and dealing with complex people issues.

Jo is passionate about helping individuals and organisations to reach their full potential, through her proven and innovative coaching style. Whilst she has been trained in the traditional coaching methods, through coaching approximately 1500 people, Jo has found her own unique style focusing on behavioural change and fundamentally changing clients' thought patterns to achieve tangible results, super-charging their performance and elevating their career or business to the next level.

Jo runs a number of inspirational leadership development stand-alone workshops which include conflict management, communication skills, effective leadership, team development, influencing skills, Neuro Linguistic Programming as well as full, year-long Leadership Programmes which incorporate revolutionary workshops backing up the learning with one-to-one coaching. All Jo's work focuses predominantly on challenging the thoughts and perceptions of participants giving them a unique blend of information and practical techniques that they can put into practice immediately.

As this book describes Jo's philosophy, it is geared towards changing people's thoughts and behaviours by teaching them to better understand themselves and the people around them, in order to achieve exceptional results.

Visit www.whatnextconsultancy.co.uk/testimonials to see for yourself the amazing feedback Jo receives on a consistent basis.

CONNECT WITH JO

Twitter: @JoBanks247

Web 1:   www.thoughtsbecomethings.co.uk

Web 2:   www.whatnextconsultancy.co.uk

Blog: www.whatnextconsultancy.co.uk/blog

THOUGHTS BECOME THINGS

Made in the USA
Charleston, SC
06 January 2016